P9-BYA-307

GROWING UP ON CAPE COD

FOUR BROTHERS

LEARNING TO STAND TALL

Don Sparrow

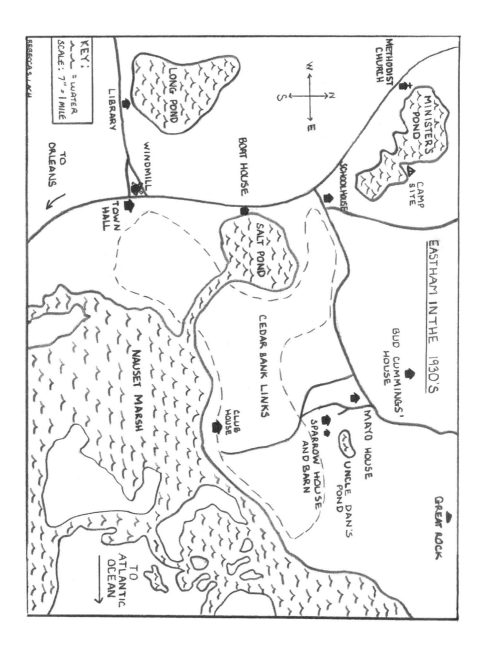

EASTHAM IN THE 1930'S

KEY:
∿ = WATER
SCALE: 7" = 1 MILE

REBECCA S. BEAL

GROWING UP ON CAPE COD

FOUR BROTHERS

LEARNING TO STAND TALL

By

Donald B. Sparrow

With Illustrations by Rebecca S. Lach

Great Oaks Publishing

Eastham, MA

Library of Congress Catalog Card Number: 99-97669

Published by the Great Oaks Publishing Co.
Box 1051
Eastham, MA 02642

Copyright © 1999 by D.B. Sparrow
All rights reserved
ISBN 0-9677008-9-2

DEDICATION

For Genevieve whose support, patience
and love have made this possible.

ACKNOWLEDGEMENTS

Jan Young's creative editorial inputs

•

Linda Weisler's contributions in formatting
and preparing the manuscript for printing

•

Rebecca Lach's charming sketches

•

Genevieve's creative suggestions
have all been vital to putting this book into its final form

TABLE OF CONTENTS

FOREWARD

This book began with a series of articles in *The Cape Codder* on the subject of growing up on Cape Cod. They tell about my boyhood experiences and those of my three brothers along with those of our Eastham neighbors and friends in the period just before World War II.

The chief characters in this story are my parents, Daniel Wilbur and Jennie Baxter (Smith) Sparrow and their four sons—Wilbur; who was born in Dec. 1917; Robert, in Sept. 1919; Donald, in June 1921 and finally Fenton in Jan. 1923. Eastham's population at that time was comprised of about 450 people and there were only a dozen boys our age in the entire town.

The map opposite the title page shows many of the areas where we played and worked. We didn't stray from these boundaries until high school. Our world was geographically small, but almost unlimited in the opportunities it presented to young boys: to get into and out of trouble, to have fun and to grow up.

I have included a brief account of our parents' and grandparents' lives but most of the stories cover the four brothers' activities over the years from roughly 1926, (my earliest memories), to the end of 1941 and Pearl Harbor.

CHAPTER 1

PROLOGUE

"Outermost cliff and solitary dune,
the plain of ocean
and the far bright rims of the world,
meadow land and marsh and ancient moor:
this is Eastham,
this is the outer Cape."

(THE OUTERMOST HOUSE, HENRY BESTON,
DOUBLEDAY, DORAN AND COMPANY, INC. 1929)

ur ancestors moved from Kent, England, to Plymouth, Massachusetts in 1636, and thence to Eastham on Cape Cod in 1653. Eastham's rich, fertile soil had attracted Plymouth residents who moved here in 1644. The area became known as the breadbasket of Massachusetts. To make way for corn and wheat fields they cleared the virgin forests, which had held and enriched the soil for centuries. By the late 1700's the soil was farmed out or had blown away and farming had become a marginal occupation.

Other ways of making a living emerged and flourished for a while. Whaling, salt-from-sea-water and coastal vessel transport all brought a measure of prosperity but each had faded or disappeared by the early 1900's. Most Cape Codders scratched a meager living from the sandy soil, dug clams and quahogs from the tidal flats, fished the deeper bay and ocean waters or, "took in each other's laundry"—usually by necessity it became a combination of all three. Many left to seek their fortune within the rapidly expanding economy of the mainland.

The fortunes of the Sparrow clan, at least my branch, ebbed and flowed along with those of the other Cape Codders. At the turn of the century our grandmother was a widow with seven children ranging in age from one to 17, struggling to survive on four acres of sandy, stony farmland. One of her sons, Daniel Wilbur Sparrow, became the head of the household at 14, stayed on the farm, married and raised his family there. He and his wife, Jennie B. Smith, a Hyannisport Cape Codder, had four boys in the five years from October 1917 to January 1923. The following tells how we lived, worked and played—exploring the ocean, dunes, "meadow land and marsh and ancient moor, the far bright rims of the world."

CHAPTER 2

THE GRANDPARENTS—WILBUR AND SOPHIA

*O*ur grandmother, a deaf mute, is left a widow with no money and seven children living on a small farm in Eastham at the turn of the century. A combination of her backbreaking labor and the help of the older children enabled the family to survive and even thrive during this difficult period.

Father's parents were both deaf mutes, in each case as a result of early childhood bouts with scarlet fever. Wilbur Norris, born in Eastham in 1854, had no formal education until he was nine years old when Dr. Edward Gallaudet, the head of Connecticut's Hartford Asylum for the Deaf and Dumb, made a tour of the New England states looking for suitable students for his school. Someone recommended that he contact a nine year old deaf and mute Eastham boy. He did so, was impressed, and invited him to come to Hartford. Several years later, Dr. Gallaudet moved to Washington D.C. to head up the school which became Gallaudet College, now a world-renowned college for the deaf. Wilbur won a scholarship that enabled him to attend the four-year College from 1872 to 1877.

Gallaudet student body in 1874. Wilbur Sparrow, second row from the front, third from the left.

A picture of the student body in 1874 reveals that bizarre dress among the younger set was just as prevalent then as it is now. Grandfather seems to have a bee stung cheek although a studio photo of the time shows no disfigurement on his thin 18-year-old face. He majored in English and left us one example of his florid, Elizabethan style—an oration written as though it was being given by Eastham's town pump on Independence Day. Following is a brief excerpt from the 1000 word essay: "Welcome most rubicund Sir! You and I have been great strangers hitherto, nor to confess the truth, will my nose be anxious for a more immediate intimacy until the fumes of your breath be a little less potent."

Wilbur graduated with a BA degree in 1877 and taught in the Kendall School, Gallaudet's middle and high school program. Sophia Weller, one of his pupils, had moved from Thurman, Maryland when she was nine years old to attend the school. Like Wilbur, she had been stricken with scarlet fever as a child and was deaf and mute. The young teacher fell in love with his slender, attractive 17-year-old student. The match appeared to have the support of all concerned because they were married in 1881 with the blessing of two officials, the Methodist Church's minister and Dr. Gallaudet, for the deaf in attendance.

Wilbur Norris Sparrow. Gallaudet College picture, 1877.

The newlyweds returned to the Cape to care for Wilbur's mother, who had been struggling to survive by herself on the farm. Two years before her husband had died in a freak accident while he and Wilbur were fishing from a dory off Nauset Beach. A large wave tore an oar from his hands and as he reached for it another heavy swell threw him against the gunnel and both men fell into the water as the boat capsized.

The son managed to reach shore, but his father had been knocked unconscious. Kept afloat by the air trapped in his oil-skins, but floating face down, he drowned before onlookers could reach him.

The return to Eastham proved to be disastrous for the young couple. A chronic ear/mastoid infection weakened Wilbur and the rough life of an Eastham farmer-fisherman was beyond his physical capabilities. In addition, he was an indifferent farmer, preferring to spend much of his time reading while his wife and children did the work. It appears he was adequate in one department; the couple produced eight children over the next 17 years. Nevertheless, Wilbur's health continued to deteriorate and he died from what was described as a brain abscess in 1898 at the early age of 44.

The young deaf and mute widow, Sophia, faced a grim future: no money, no man, seven children aged one to 17, (one had died in infancy), and no expectation of help from relatives or public agencies. But she was used to hard times; the couple had been less than affluent ever since moving back to the farm. The older children were already working, the girls as domestics and the boys shoveling snow, helping to maintain town roads or farming their stony, sandy four acres on the rim of Nauset Marsh. When his own father died, my father was only ten but he worked along with the older ones. When he turned 14 he quit school and, in effect, became the male head of the family.

Sophia Weller Sparrow with family dog, Gyp, in 1910, the year she died.

Sophia was not idle. She took in washing, sewed button-holes into trousers for H. K. Cumming's pants factory in Orleans, (75 cents per dozen pair—no zippers) and provided meals for itinerant peddlers. An expert seamstress, she sewed for many ladies in town and made all the family's clothes as well.

Judging from her wedding gown on display in the Eastham Historical Society's Swift Daley House Museum, she was slender, about five feet tall and couldn't have weighed more than 100 pounds. A 1910 picture shows a handsome woman of 64 years with high cheekbones and eyelids with an Oriental crease (called a Mongoloid fold). These characteristics hint at some Indian blood in the family background, a trait I have not been able to document but hope is true.

My grandmother was able to make sounds but not form words. Our cousin, Evelyn Mayo, told me that the children sometimes made fun of her when she tried to communicate in a high-pitched mumble. In the picture she looks rather somber but Evelyn described her as always smiling and jovial, with a mischievous streak. Playing with the small children, she might lift her skirt above her ankles and do an impromptu clog dance about the kitchen.

By 1910 most of the children were self-supporting and Sophia was able to gain a degree of freedom from the grinding routine. Tragically, that same year she fell on the cellar stairs, broke several ribs and died of complications from a punctured lung. It was only 12 years since her husband's death but those were critical years for her children. Working unbelievably long hours, she saw that they were fed, clothed, took music lessons, went to church and attended at least grammar school.

GROWING UP ON CAPE COD

CHAPTER 3

AUNTS AND UNCLES

ophia's children learn to survive with the cards life has dealt them.

When Sophia's husband died, their oldest child, Marion, was 17, engaged to be married, and destined to become a mother herself within a couple of years. Her prospective husband, Warren Mayo, was building a house not more than 100 yards from the homestead to entice the beautiful, (I'm told), young girl into marriage. Over the next 25 years she had seven children, spanning two generations—her first was close to the same age as her youngest sister, Nora, and her last two boys, Carleton and Kenneth, were in the same age group as the four Sparrow boys. Living so close we spent as much time in our cousins' house as in our own.

Frank, the next oldest, was 15 and already working full time to help support the family. He stayed with his mother for four or five years and then married and moved to Vermont to seek his fortune. The move was ill advised. He just exchanged one depressed area for another, living on a rocky and unproductive farm. Vermont, like Cape Cod, ultimately became a popular place for retirement homes and wealthy vacation retreats but much too late for Frank to participate in the economic boom.

Frank was able to leave Eastham because the next oldest children, Rosalind and Dan, were now 16 and 14, capable of helping Sophia to raise the younger children. My Aunt Rosie was a hard worker much like her mother. In her early teens she worked as a domestic in affluent homes on the Cape. She continued to follow this profession, never marrying, until she died at 33 of what the death certificate describes as "Intestinal Nephritis, Myocarditis." Her younger sister Nora told me she collapsed at work, lay in a fetal position for three days and then died.

Daniel, or Dan as everyone called him, would eventually became the father of the four boys whose lives are the center of this story. His younger brother, Robert, graduated from Orleans High School, completed the two-year course at the Massachusetts Nautical Training School and had a distinguished maritime career. The youngest girls, Anne and Nora, finished high school and left Eastham. Anne married a marine engineer, George Sibley, a Training School classmate of her brother Rob. The couple met when Rob brought him to Eastham for a home cooked dinner. According to family legend, during their courtship days George persuaded the captain of his ship to bring the vessel close enough to the Eastham Coast Guard Station to send a semiphore flag message to his fiance. Anne's brother-in-law, Warren Mayo, a Coastguardsman at the station, interpreted the signals and transmitted her reply—his proposal of marriage and her acceptance. George left the sea in the

Aunt Rosie,
about 1918

Aunt Nora, seated right and Cousin Evelyn Mayo, standing second from right, with neighbors, the Brown children. About 1910.

early 30's and returned to Eastham, a Depression victim, I suspect. The family remained in town permanently.

Nora graduated from Hyannis Normal School, taught for a few years and married a Chatham businessman, Charles Harding. He was a good provider, at one time serving as president of a local bank. It seemed to us that Aunt Nora was overly conscious of their affluent position. During one Sunday visit I remember her describing an elegant restaurant where they had dined. Mother said, "I understand it's very expensive." Aunt Nora merely replied "Yes," with a somewhat superior smile.

All of Sophia's children inherited their mother's prominent cheekbones, traces of a Mongoloid fold on the outer portions of their eyelids, erect carriage and enormous energy— a vital and striking group of people. With the exception of Frank, they stayed on warm, friendly terms and exchanged

Sunday visits frequently. Those visits were never dull. Even though their parents had been deaf and mute, when the siblings got together an outsider had to fight to get a word in edgewise.

We didn't see much of Frank and his family, visits in either direction were not frequent, and to we boys, never seemed particularly cordial. As an adult I learned that in his youth father's relationship with Frank had not been smooth. Aunt Nora told me that in their teens Frank beat his younger brother severely, once knocking him unconscious for several minutes with a blow to the head. She theorized that this may have been the cause of a medical problem that started in his mid 30's and clouded his later life.

CHAPTER 4

PARENTS—DAN AND JENNIE

*T*he busiest man in town gets by with a remarkable array of money-making activities, modernizes the farmhouse, marries Jennie B. Smith and fathers four boys in the next five years.

Even as a young teenager, Dan developed an astonishing range of activities as he struggled to keep the family going. He worked the family farm, fished, dug clams, poled for eels in the winter, shoveled snow and worked on the public roads.

Father working on Route 6, in Eastham, with the Overlook Inn in the background.

13

He and his team of horses helped to pave what is now Route 6 in Eastham. In addition, he drove duck and geese hunters to the Nauset Marshes and the West Shore, plowed for other farmers and looked after vacation homes in the off-season.

Despite this grueling schedule, he found time for an active social life and public service as well. He was an exceptionally good dancer and frequently won Waltz or Schodische contests. His sister Nora, an infant when their father died, remembered that he took her to a dance once when she was "no bigger than a hop toad," and whirled her around the floor. A contemporary, Abbie Collins, recalled that Dan drove the snappiest horse and buggy and dressed in the latest fashion. "What a handsome man he was," she once remarked with a wistful smile. Later, he filled a number of town offices, including a term as selectman. A picture of him in his early 20's shows a muscular, broad shouldered six-footer who carried himself with a back as straight as a ramrod.

Daniel Wilbur Sparrow in his mid-20's, about 1915.

By 1916 the youngest children had left home and for the first time in his life Dan was alone, without family responsibilities. That year he met Jennie Baxter Smith, a Hyannis native and Hyannis Normal School graduate who had moved to Eastham to serve as intermediate teacher in the old, three-room school. Jennie B., (as one of her students, Sadie Flint, and many of her friends called her), had dark hair, brown eyes and in the school teacher uniform of the day—ruffled white blouse and tightly belted long skirt—she presented a most attractive picture. Within a few months' of arriving in town, she caught the eye of the

Jennie Baxter Smith, upper right, with her parents and brothers, about 1910.

eligible bachelor, they married and she moved into the family homestead. Dan and Jennie didn't have the house to themselves for long. Over the next five years they produced four sons: Daniel Wilbur Jr., Robert Weller, Donald Baxter (the author) and Fenton Bearse. Four growing boys created a harrowing work schedule for both parents.

Dan and Jennie in 1924. Boys from left—Donald, Wilbur, Robert and Fenton in mother's arms.

15

Ever the entrepreneur, father tried to escape the farmer/ handyman life in 1924 by buying George Clark's general store off Samoset Road. The building housed the only store in that section of Eastham, as well as the post office and, for a time, the town library. It was located by the railroad tracks, across from the depot on a road called, prophetically, Know Nothing Road. Dan paid cash, all his savings, for the building. Then, a day after the sale became final, and before he had obtained insurance, the store burned to the ground. With his savings gone and a wife and four small children to support, the family faced a difficult future.

Help came from one of his long time gunning camp customers, a United Shoe Machinery executive, Herbert Winslow. Mr. Winslow wrote a check for the full amount of Dan's loss and said, "Pay me back when you can." No contract was signed, a handshake sufficed. It took two years for father to discharge the obligation, working harder than ever.

The man who dropped out of high school to work the family farm continued to develop a wide range of occupations. In 1928, when I was seven and becoming aware of what he did all day, he supervised an 18-hole private golf course, sold asparagus and turnips to the Boston produce markets, served as caretaker for several lower Cape summer estates, acted as the local representative for Kohler electric generating plants and guided duck and geese hunters on the ocean and West Shore beaches. When time hung heavily on his hands, he went to New Bedford, picked up a truckload of green bananas, hung them in our basement, and sold the ripened fruit to local merchants.

Like most Cape Codders of the time, he also kept a couple of cows, a horse, a flock of hens, and a pig, and maintained a small truck garden. Mother had the four of us boys to keep her busy but also helped with asparagus bunching, preserved

The Sparrow boys after a pineapple clip haircut. From left, Fenton, Donald, Robert and Wilbur.

garden produce for winter consumption and managed the golf course accounts.

Another of father's skills should be mentioned: on top of everything else he was the family barber. All concerned hated this venture. Haircuts almost always ended with each of us squirming and crying as the hand-operated clippers pulled at our hair and father cursed and yelled at us to sit still. In order to make the summers more pleasant he gave us what we called a pineapple clip, as close to the skull as possible so that our heads were as bare as a pineapple by the day school vacation started. A photograph of the time typically shows Wilbur and Robert with bald heads gleaming in the June sun. Although Fenton and I hid our heads, I'm sure that both of us also had the end-of-school treatment.

During the 1920's father expanded his house to accommodate his growing family. It had been built in the early 1800's, a classic, small, one-and-a-half story Cape, but had been modified and expanded over the years—a full basement replaced a root cellar, a kitchen ell, another ell on the opposite end for a parlor, two shed dormers to make a full second story, a bay window on the dining room and a porch (or piazza as we

Sparrow family homestead, about 1920, prior to addition of dormers, front piazza and West wing for parlor. Aunt Annie and mother with Wilbur in front.

called it), across the front. It was a comfortable, four-bed-room house but the materials of the new construction gave us problems. Recovered saltworks boards had been used in some of the remodeling. Iron nails in the salt-encrusted boards quickly rusted and left only reddish brown stained spots. The loosely fastened house swayed back and forth at least six inches in a heavy wind, making us a bit uneasy as we lay in bed trying to sleep.

Wood used in the kitchen flooring swelled excessively in humid weather and so the floor developed a strange configuration in summer. It resembled a corrugated roof with two feet between crests and a depth of one or two inches from crest to trough. Our mother groaned over the housekeeping difficulties this created but we liked it. Liquid spills were easier to clean up and it made play with marbles or toy cars far more interesting.

Modern conveniences such as indoor plumbing, central heating and electricity were added in the 1920's as family finances improved. Hot water radiators with convection circulation throughout the house replaced the only downstairs hot air register. This was a mixed blessing. Our bedrooms were somewhat warmer but I missed standing over the register in my flannel nightgown, allowing it to balloon out with hot air and then rushing upstairs to a cold bed.

Electrification didn't come to our section of the Cape until the early 1930's so father installed a Kohler lighting plant about five years before public power was available. It delivered alternating current and so the first light in the evening turned on the gasoline-powered generator and it shut down when the last light was extinguished. He reserved the honor of turning on the first bulb and we had to wait for close to total darkness before he would relent and

click the switch. Similarly, all lights went out when he retired so flashlights were standard equipment if we wished to read in bed—and we always did.

In all his toil and thriftiness, father allowed himself one extravagance: the luxury of a new Auburn sedan automobile every two years. It was always cash on the barrel-head; father thought it foolhardy, even immoral, to buy on credit and pay interest. The Auburn was used almost exclusively for the family Sunday drive. We either visited relatives or explored Cape Cod and beyond. Draw bridges spanned the Cape

Father in his first car, a 1912 Model T Ford.

19

Sparrow brothers standing straight, except for Fenton. From left, Robert, Fenton, Donald and Wilbur.

Cod Canal in those days and it seemed that the bridge was always up when we returned from an off-Cape trip and got caught in hour long traffic jams: a forerunner of today's massive summer tie-ups at the bridges.

We probably saw more of our father during those Sunday rides than at any other time during the week. It provided the opportunity for us to get to know each other—and for him to lecture us. The need to be honest in our dealings with others was drilled into us. We were always commanded to stand straight when in public. In the picture showing the four of us in our everyday attire, posed before one of the prized Auburns, we appear to be practicing standing up straight, (although Fenton apparently had not yet gotten the word). So ingrained were these two orders, ("Stand straight, Be straight"), I once thought of naming this book "Growing Up Straight". But then the term took on a completely different meaning—although the title would be totally accurate by any interpretation.

CHAPTER 5

THE BARN

 an and Jennie work and their sons work, play, and learn something about the facts of life.

During much of the year the family spent more time in the barn than in the house. It was a comfortable place, serving as a recreation room, gym, laboratory, classroom and "wood-shed," as well as a work place. It was a classic Cape Cod saltbox, 25 feet by 35 feet, built into the side of a hill so that the main entrance led into the second of three floors. Double doors, big enough to accommodate a fully loaded hay rick, hung on iron wheels, which traveled along a metal track. Haymows occupied the upper level and the basement held storage sheds and a manure pit. The middle, operating, floor had a long bench with three asparagus bunchers, a grain bin, a work bench with cabinets, and a tool chest. A smaller door on rollers led back to the horse and cow stalls, a 50-gallon wood-en barrel drinking trough and a trap door to the manure pit.

Over its 100 years of use, the building had accumulated a rich, pungent aroma with overtones that changed with the seasons. The basic odors of pine lumber overlaid with vapors

Sparrow boys in front of their barn.

rising from the manure pit were enhanced in late spring by the sweet smell of freshly mowed and dried hay. In early July the aroma was spiced with ground oranges and lemons and laced with molasses (our primitive asparagus pesticide), and in August the sharp odor of pyrethrum and petroleum distillate, hand sprayed onto cows and horses to provide protection from the clouds of voracious flies.

The barn job we liked least was cleaning out the manure pit. Every spring we put on hip boots and pitchforked the accumulated manure onto a cart and then spread it on the asparagus beds. Other barn chores included pitching hay up to the haymows, feeding the animals and helping with the preparation of asparagus for market.

It's not surprising that I remember much more clearly the fun times. The barn was the scene of most of our rainy day recreational activities. Repairing Sears Roebuck balloon tire bicycles took a great deal of our time, especially those New Departure, pedal-operated, coaster brakes. This complex device was made up of what seemed to be hundreds of little pieces and hardly ever worked properly. We took them apart and ended up with a multitude of parts spread all over the barn floor. After reassembly, we always had a few parts left over, but happily, the "repaired" brakes seemed to work just as well as the brand new ones.

The spaces between the overhead, exposed beams were full of plastering lathes that had been salvaged from the "Montclair" when the 143-foot, three-masted schooner carrying two million of the lathes ran aground and foundered on Nauset Beach in 1927. Many Eastham barns were similarly equipped, and we, and our friends found all sorts of uses for the three-foot slats—swords, boomerangs, toy boats or just plain whittling stock.

Barn swallows nested in the spaces where the barn door rolled on its tracks and this irritated my father mightily. The birds created a terrible mess and their nests clogged the rollers. Because he had to clean out the nests frequently he encouraged us to shoot them with our BB guns and we became quite proficient at this.

We experimented with dried weeds and other agricultural residues as tobacco substitutes. Our make-believe tobaccos all tasted terrible—corn silk, grapevine cuttings, "coffee plant" weed. We were always on the lookout for a chance to try the real thing. Ten-year-old Fenton came home one afternoon appearing pale and drawn. Asked what he had been doing, he replied, "Oh, just playing in Fulcher's barn." As he said this, he unzipped his jacket and out fell a partially smoked cigar. Mother struggled to suppress a grin as she threw the cigar in the kitchen stove and scolded the sheepish Fenton.

We spent as little time as possible in the barn during the height of the August fly season. Screens were not practical on the huge door opening and so the smelly fly spray and fly coils were used to control the pests. When fully extended, the coils stretched out to three feet of paper covered with brown, sticky fly poison. They were quickly loaded with flies, but it was a losing battle—the flies bred much faster than we could put out fresh fly paper to vanquish their offspring. Spray was equally ineffective. Once, in desperation, our parents offered to pay us, and our friends a nickel per cup of dead flies. With this financial incentive, we wielded swatters with great enthusiasm and succeeded in somewhat reducing the fly population. However, the program collapsed when our neighbor Bob Watson, always a creative entrepreneur, was discovered selling cups of raisins from Bud and Millie's kitchen with a top dressing of dead flies.

The barn was also a place for doling out discipline. When we misbehaved badly, our father would order us to the "woodshed," promising "the thrashing of your life." He always cooled down on the 25-foot walk from the house to the barn and we got a loud, long lecture but none of us ever received the thrashing. The verbal furor was probably as effective as the physical punishment might have been.

Once when I was in my early teens, all four of us were ordered to the barn for a very puzzling discussion. I later learned that one of the neighborhood boys had gotten into a situation which was then regarded much more seriously than it is now. Our mother must have insisted that father tell us something about the facts of life so that we might avoid a similar fate.

Seriously and nervously, he meandered about in comments on school, farm work and the weather, his face growing redder and redder. Finally, after a long silence, he blurted out, "You know your friend, ___ ___, has gotten into very serious trouble and I don't want any of you to do anything like that." We all solemnly promised never to do such a thing, but he hadn't told us the nature of the terrible deed, and I didn't have the slightest idea as to what he was talking about. Afterwards, the more worldly and older brother, Robert, told me that our friend had contracted a social disease and had to undergo an extensive period of medication.

Yet the basic facts of life were not too mysterious to anyone growing up among farm animals. When I was six or seven, I observed father loading one of our cows into his Brockway truck.

"Oh, he's just taking her for a ride", Mother explained. I was greatly impressed with father's kindness and commented to that effect at the dinner table. He reddened, choked, cleared his throat several times and struggled to change the subject. Robert, again, took me aside after dinner and explained that the real purpose of the joy ride was a tryst with Obed Fulcher's bull.

The barn provided us with much information on many subjects, some of it useful only in bar room bets or Trivial Pursuit. For example, does a hen lay an egg standing or sitting? Fenton and I speculated on this question one summer day when we had nothing else to do. We made ourselves inconspicuous in the hen house and waited for what seemed an eternity. The hen stood up, an egg fell into the nesting hay, and we knew, for sure.

We also learned what happens when a cow eats a certain weed or green apples, if a horse slept standing or lying down, if chickens eat lobster—and much more. The answers were in the barn.

CHAPTER 6

UNCLE DAN'S POND

 he four seasons around a Cape Cod kettle
pond come and go and four boys learn to
appreciate the advantages of each season.

The pond behind our barn was the focus of our outdoor
play in early childhood. This quarter-mile wide body of water
was too shallow and mucky for swimming, but we found
plenty to do around the shore. My three brothers and I sailed

Uncle Dan's pond with barn in background.

toy boats, sank tin cans with stones or BB guns, caught frogs and, when our folks weren't looking, waded out into the pond —testing the theory that the bottom was made of quicksand, (it was not). Arrowwood shrubs lined the shores and we followed the Indian practice of using its strong and supple stalks for bows and arrows. Trails through the shrubs made an ideal arena for cowboy and Indian games. Black snakes liked the area too, because they could travel through the upper branches, gliding from twig to twig, propelling themselves with a wriggling, side-to-side motion. They were able to speed along at such a pace we had trouble keeping up, if we really wanted to catch them.

One of the earliest signals of spring was the high-pitched call of hordes of little tree toads—"peepers" or "pink-winks". The shallow edges of the pond were alive with tadpoles, which turned to frogs before our fascinated eyes. Occasionally, we could hear the distinctive mating call of a stakedriver (American Bittern). I never saw the shy, swamp-dwelling bird, but its call sounded to us as though someone were driving a hardwood stake into frozen ground. An Audubon Society listing confirms my childhood memory— "an elusive bird with a mating cry which can only be described as the sound of a stake being driven into hard ground".

As spring turned to summer, a variety of wildflowers appeared. Clear blue iris and two kinds of pond lilies—heavy, graceless, yellow "cowslips" and exquisite, delicately perfumed, pure white flowers lined the shores and shallow lagoons. Clouds of dragonflies darted about and we were carefully mute, believing the old-wive's tale, "If you swear, they'll sew your lips shut".

Many varieties of turtles inhabited the pond, black mud turtles, brightly patterned box turtles, and large ugly snappers. Once we came upon a snapper laying her eggs in a sandy bank near the pond and recovered 20 to 30 of the white ping-pong shaped eggs with leather-like shells. For years I took my two sons to the same spot, hoping to come upon the same wondrous event. We were never there at the right time, but I haven't given up: now my grandchildren help me look.

Dome-shaped structures of reed and mud gave away the location of muskrat families making the pond their home. Sometimes at sunset, when the wind died, we could see a perfect, V-shaped wake as a muskrat made its way across the water, the V stretching from shore to shore in the mirror-smooth, sunset-red tinged surface of the pond.

In the fall, the bare redberry bush branches were covered with brilliant red fruit flaming against the clear blue sky. A haunting call drew our attention to great flocks of Canadian geese as they headed south, sometimes making a stop on our little pond.

Skating was the only activity around the pond in winter. The very shallow pond froze early in a uniform sheet so that it provided the best skating in the neighborhood. We became enthusiastic, if amateurish, hockey players. One year we even challenged a bigger and heavier Orleans team. Despite their weight advantage, we walloped them because our goalie wore homemade pads and fended off the puck with a stick made from a one by six board. The Orleans team had nothing like our man's sophisticated equipment.

We built great bonfires on the ice for skating parties at night and roasted hot dogs and marshmallows over the embers. I was always mystified that the fire didn't melt its way right through the water and sputter out. When we had an extended freeze the ice developed cracks to relieve stresses in the smooth layer on the pond. Lying in bed at night we could hear the scary, tearing, resonating boom when a crack started and made its way across the pond.

Uncle Dan's pond is still there, made smaller by 50 years of encroaching reeds and other swampy vegetation, but still a stop over point for south-bound geese, and still ablaze with redberries and crimson foliage in the fall. A National Seashore bicycle trail runs by its shores, close to the bushes where we cut arrowwood branches for bows and arrows and built a network of Indian trails. Now, I walk the bicycle path, listen to the springtime pink-winks and keep a watchful eye on the bank where the snapper laid its eggs.

CHAPTER 7

WHEN CHRISTMAS WAS FOR CHILDREN

anta arrives by the front door, Tom Mix makes an appearance and mother finally receives a Christmas gift.

I remember when Christmas holiday festivities were largely for the benefit of children. Without the benefit of store Santas and television it was much easier for children of the 20's and 30's to sustain belief in the childhood Christmas myth. Santa's arrival at the Eastham Town Hall on Christmas Eve didn't shake our faith. We knew that it was really Freddy Gill behind that cotton batting beard passing out gifts to the children and that the genuine Santa would come to our house later that night.

When I was about five I began to wonder how Santa managed to enter our house with no fireplace. Mother suggested the front door and we believed her because we never locked it. In fact, we had no key for the lock. Snow covered the ground that Christmas Eve and in the morning we saw sled runner grooves and tiny little hoof marks in the snow leading right up to our front door. I never learned how father accomplished this trick without leaving his own footprints in the

31

Sparrow boys on a snowless Christmas morning. Wilbur and Robert wearing their roll-collar, Christmas present sweaters.

snow, but my faith was restored for another year.

Opening even one present was strictly forbidden until after breakfast. Our parents used their once-a-year clout to force us to eat breakfast, wash the dishes and tidy up the house first. That morning meal was a long, drawn out affair. We wolfed down our bacon and eggs and then waited impatiently as our parents had a second and then a third cup of coffee. Only after the dishes were dried and the floor dust-free could we assemble in the parlor and wait for father to pass out the gifts, one at a time.

Every year we each got one major gift such as a sled, pair of skates, bicycle or a scooter. One year my big gift was a hand-cranked projector and one reel of film. The Tom Mix cowboy short lasted two to six minutes, depending on how fast we cranked. The hero in his big, white, Stetson cowboy hat and bulky, sheepskin covered chaps swaggered into a frontier saloon and confronted the black-hatted villain and his evil gang. The battle was a short one. The bad guys came tumbling out the doors and windows as he cleared out the bar single-handedly. Tom Mix emerged, hopped onto his horse and rode away into the sunset. If we cranked too fast, the saloon exploded with flying bodies and Tom's galloping horse bounded away like a jackrabbit. Too slow and the villains cartwheeled lazily through the air as they were ejected from the bar, and horse with rider leisurely ambled towards the horizon. The same reel was played over and over for several months, and we never got another.

In accordance with father's family custom, only the children got presents at Christmas, and mother bravely went along. Occasionally, she made reference to gifts other women received, and finally one year, father had something for her— a pair of scissors. She burst into tears and sobbed for some time. I was never sure whether she cried because at long last she got a gift, or because of its impersonal nature. Next year the four of us pooled our resources and bought her a bathrobe for Christmas. This time there was no doubt as to the reason for the tears.

Every Christmas, Grandpa Smith and Aunt Phoebe would arrive from Hyannis as the boys cleaned up wrapping paper and other debris (another must before playing with the toys). Mother's father was a small man, a shade over five feet tall, who wore a perpetually sad expression behind a handlebar moustache. His wife had died a few years before and he led a lonely life, living by himself in the large family home. Aunt Phoebe lived about a mile away on the Smith family farm with two of her sisters. The youngest of a family of eight children, the three old maids had stayed home to care for their elderly parents and ended up stuck on the farm.

Mother was Aunt Phoebe's favorite niece so she visited us a lot. Her usual Christmas attire was a gray or grayish-blue, flowered silk dress with starched white cuffs and collar.

She was even shorter than her brother and wore an iron gray wig, thick glasses, a nearly completely ineffective hearing aid, and walked with a cane. Despite the collection of assorted infirmities she was as lively as a cricket, interested in everything, and doted on the four of us. We were always glad to see her, but father was less enthusiastic. Two of her dinner dishes—hot water with a splash of skimmed milk, (called cambric tea), and soured milk, (before yogurt became so popular)—almost drove him from the table.

Grandpa Smith's visits were more welcome to father. His arrival provided an excuse for him to dip a couple of tumblers of red wine from a barrel stashed in the barn, hidden there because Prohibition was in force. Grandpa drained his glass in one long swallow and wiped his moustache with the back of his hand. He never asked for another and was never offered a second. Many years later I learned that in his youth he had an alcohol problem and allowed himself the twice-a-year, Thanksgiving and Christmas, glass at our house.

Competing for our attention along with the Christmas presents was an array of pre-dinner delicacies: walnut-stuffed dates rolled on powdered sugar, dried figs, mixed nuts, ribbon candy and peanut brittle. Filling our pockets with as much as we could grab on the fly, we made our get-away to play outside. Hunger brought us back for dinner, served promptly at one o'clock. Father carved the sausage-stuffing-turkey with great ceremony and the usual jokes about the part over the fence last, also known as the Pope's nose in our fiercely Protestant household. Usually a thoughtful and generous man, father selected the portion he favored first, a drumstick, carefully carved it and set it aside before serving the rest of the table. No one objected; we regarded it as his patriarchal right.

After dinner, stuffed with turkey, an unreasonable assortment of vegetables and the desserts we hadn't "saved room for," we went out again to try the new toys. We headed for Uncle Dan's pond or, if there was enough snow, the good sliding hill next to Salt Pond where the National Seashore Visitor's Center is now located. From the peak overlooking the Pond we could shoot down parallel to the shore and with a hard right, slide out onto the frozen surface.

At sundown, we headed back home for more food and to say goodbye to the relatives. The older people had spent the afternoon "resting" and were in no mood for a big supper. After a weak stab at the piles of leftovers, the guests struggled into heavy overcoats and departed, Grandpa Smith with a perfunctory pat on the head, and Aunt Phoebe with a shy, chaste peck on the cheek. With a notable lack of enthusiasm, father loaded them into his cold car for the two hour round trip drive to their homes in Hyannis and back (nearby relatives had brought them down to Eastham).

As I grow nostalgic over Christmases past, I think, "Wouldn't it be great if the day were again only for children?" and, patting my expanding middle, "Wouldn't it be great to be able to eat like that again?"

CHAPTER 8

FARM CHORES

*T*he four brothers become accustomed to hard work on the family farm—helping to grow asparagus and turnips and to prepare firewood for the kitchen stove.

We grew up during the Great Depression when the Cape's economy, like the entire world economy was in rough shape. Eastham had experienced a steady decline in population of about 3 percent per year beginning in the mid 19th century — a trend which didn't reverse until World War II boosted the entire nation out of the Depression. As a sign of the times, when we started to make money from odd jobs, our parents encouraged us to put the major portion of the earnings into our own bank account. The purpose was two-fold—to teach us the "value of money" and to enable us "to get an education." An education would be our passport to escape from the stagnant economy and lack of opportunity on the Cape.

Outside work for money didn't excuse us from working at home. As young boys our major chores were helping with asparagus and turnips and cutting wood for the kitchen stove. The harvesting season for asparagus began around the last two weeks of April and was over by July fourth. The stalks grew three or four inches a day in warm weather, and we were routed out of bed at sunrise every day to harvest the three beds (about three acres). Typically, it took us, and a hired hand two hours to finish the daily cutting and bring in the "grass" to the barn for bunching.

Our cutting tools were a wooden handled knife with a rectangular blade two inches wide by seven inches long and a file. The square end needed to be sharpened frequently as we walked the rows so by the end of the season it was at least three inches shorter. Each cut had to be made in a very precise fashion. The knife was inserted into the soil adjacent to the five to seven inch stalk so as to avoid severing the immature, below ground growth. Once inserted into the ground three or four inches the knife blade was pushed over and down at a 30-degree angle to make the cut. This technique was so thoroughly drilled into us that even now I can't cut a weed root or other underground growth any differently. The proper asparagus cutting stance has the legs straight and a 90 degree

Sparrow family cutting asparagus. Uncle Dan's pond and Sparrow barn in background.

bend at the waist, straightening up only to sharpen our knife or swat flies. The younger boys, before being allowed to wield a knife, had the job of picking up the handfuls of cut asparagus in woven wood baskets, 25-30 pounds when full, and bringing them back to the truck.

The last of the three asparagus beds was within sight of our house, across a small pond. Mother started the bacon frying as soon as she spotted us and when the wind was right the aroma floating across the pond drove us mad as we hurried to finish the last few rows to get to the breakfast table. Breakfast started with cereal and cut fruit lathered with heavy cream; this was followed by bacon and eggs, the whites set by basting with hot bacon fat. Homemade bread, butter and jam accompanied the bacon and eggs, all washed down with whole milk, Postum or Ovaltine. Thus fortified we rushed off to school.

After breakfast, mother and hired hands bunched the asparagus. In this process two strips of red tape were placed in a set of open iron jaws and the bunch constructed by laying in spears. To complete the bunch she closed the jaws with a foot operated treadle, tied the tapes and sliced the protruding butt ends. She used to tell us that she spent her spring mornings rocking a cradle with one foot and pushing the treadle with the other. The product was attractive, perfectly symmetrical with the outside spear tips curved in, dark green at the top, shading to light green with traces of white showing at the base and held together with the bright red tape. Crates of 24 bunches weighed about 50 pounds and we shipped eight to ten crates a day to Boston markets.

The period from early May to the Fourth of July was the busiest time for asparagus, but it required attention at other times also. When the cutting ended the stalks grew up to form ferns six feet high. Weeds had to be controlled—with a cultivator pulled by our broad-backed horse Jerry, one of us riding bare back, legs sticking out almost horizontally, or by hand when the ferns became too thick to allow Jerry between the rows. This was a most unpleasant task in the hot summer weather as we battled greenhead and flatiron flies, stripped to the waist, crawling through the muggy, airless vegetation.

In winter we hammered together the crates used to ship the asparagus to market. The pre-cut components were of low-grade hard wood and split readily if the nails were not perfectly placed. We learned to drive a nail with accuracy and power.

Asparagus bugs and other insect pests were controlled during and after the cutting season with a homemade insecticide. We mixed a lethal combination of mash, molasses, ground-up citrus fruits and Paris Green, a copper salt of arsenic. Bugs disappeared when we hand-spread the crumbly mixture on the rows. We washed our hands thoroughly after this duty and assumed the customers rinsed their vegetables prior to cooking.

Turnips fit in nicely with asparagus because the seeds were planted early in July and the plants matured in the fall. We disliked thinning and weeding the growing plants but the really unpleasant task came late in fall at harvesting time after the first frost. We pulled the five-to-eight-inch diameter purple topped, white turnip, shaved the small roots with a razor sharp, six-inch knife, tossed it in the air, caught it by the cleaned end and lopped off the leaves. Our flimsy brown cotton gloves, intended to keep our hands warm, were soaked in short order and our icy fingers became numb. It's a miracle that none of us lost a finger to the murderous knife.

Cutting pine trees and sawing the logs to make fuel wood for our kitchen stove was a two-season, spring-fall exercise. We felled the trees early in the spring before the sap rose and then hauled them to the house and cut them into stove lengths in the late fall. Father had a saw table with a four-foot diameter blade driven by a pulley off his tractor. The 20-foot long looped leather belt made a soft, slapping noise as it traveled, competing with the whine of the saw.

In reducing the logs to firewood, father manned the saw table and the boys hauled the whole logs to the saw. As the blade bit into the log, the whine became a high-pitched screech, probably contributing to my present, ever increasing hearing loss. The oldest boy held the projecting end and threw the severed, 18-inch piece on to a pile. When all the logs were cut, we carted the wood to the house and stored it in the basement. At the end of the day our hands were covered with sticky pine pitch and we were dizzy with the rich, aromatic aroma of the sawn pine wood. It was hard work but enjoyable too.

Mother's role was as nurse—extracting splinters from fingers and sawdust from eyes and worrying about the safety of all of us. The process wouldn't have passed a current OSHA inspection, but miraculously, not one of us were ever seriously injured in all those years of chores using saws and sharp blades. The need for care, around the saw, was drilled into us by both parents. Father liked to exhibit a damaged finger, which had been badly cut by the rotating saw blade in his youth.

Winter was the time for us to relax a bit. Aside from hammering asparagus boxes together, keeping the wood box full and shoveling the 100-yard-long driveway after a snow storm, all we had to do was school and homework. It was father's slow time too. His major job, caretaker of a golf course, required only maintenance work at this time of the year. His boss sometimes gave him an off-season project. One year he was supplied with 100 blocks of balsa wood and asked to make duck decoys. We all helped with the whittling and it was one of our most pleasant winters.

CHAPTER 9

CEDAR BANK LINKS

ather cares for an 18-hole private golf course that existed in Eastham from 1928 to 1948. Invitation-only guests included two of America's greatest golfers, Francis Ouimet and Bobby Jones.

One of father's more important jobs was as caretaker of an 18-hole private golf course called Cedar Bank Links. The owner and sole user of the course was a wealthy Boston financier, Quincy Adams Shaw. In 1925, then in his middle 50's, Shaw had been discharged after ten years of treatment for a mental breakdown in McLean Hospital outside of Boston. Doctors at McLean told him that if he wanted to stay out of the hospital he must find an avocation that would absorb all of his free time and never be completed. Friends persuaded him to build a golf course on family-owned land in Eastham. He arrived, driving a bright red Stutz Bearcat roadster, sporting a gingery red beard, which reached to his knees, and was accompanied by an attendant from McLean. He was a well-built, muscular six-footer, balding, with a controlled manner and a serious, pensive expression. The family already

Aerial view of Cedar Bank Links in 1928.

owned a "cottage" in Eastham which became his clubhouse—
six bedrooms, a 40-foot long living room with a vaulted ceiling and a restaurant sized kitchen. It was located on Cedar
Bank, a 60-foot bluff with a stunning view of Nauset Marsh
and the Atlantic Ocean beyond.

Shaw spent months walking the property and selecting a
layout for his 18-hole course. Local workers, my father
among them, were hired to construct the course. Our horse,
Jerry, and a scoop were the only earth-moving equipment.
They dug bunkers and accomplished minor rearrangements of
the countryside, but the contours of the finished, 6,500-yard,
par-72 "links" (a Scottish word for sand hills, especially
along the seashore) were largely sculpted by nature. While
using the scoop father unearthed hundreds of arrowheads and
other Indian artifacts such as a corn grinding pestle 15 inches
long and worn glassy smooth at the working end.

Mr. Shaw's health continued to improve during the three-year construction project. The clubhouse cook reported that he found red beard trimmings on the bathroom floor almost every day. By the time the course was completed in 1928, the beard was gone and Mr. Shaw resumed responsibility for managing the family investments. The Shaw money came from the Calumet and Hecla copper mines in Upper Peninsula Michigan. Mr. Shaw's father was one of the principals in the development of those extremely profitable facilities. His only son could afford the hobby which helped to restore him to good mental health.

He was extremely proud of his course. A 1928 *Boston Evening Transcript* article described it as, "One of the finest natural layouts in the world". Every green was on a high point commanding a view of the marshes with the barrier dunes and Atlantic Ocean in the background or adjacent to a body of fresh water. The natural hazards were used to maximum advantage. Players had to approach many greens with a shot that skirted or was aimed directly towards the marsh, Salt Pond or a fresh water pond.

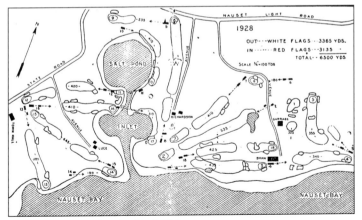

Schematic layout of Cedar Bank Links.

Most of the holes offered unusual challenges. The fourth, where the fairway sloped sharply to the right and toward the marsh, was particularly vicious. A sliced drive kicked to the right and the ball rolled down the hill and into the water. Once, when caddying, I searched a pool left by the receding tide below number four fairway and found a golf ball sharing the water with a stranded two foot pollack. In dispatching the fish with a putter, I may have established a first in angling equipment.

Another unusual hole, the 150-yard eleventh, should have been one of the easiest. However, players had to drive from a bluff overlooking an inlet to another bluff on the other side, and as a psychologically intimidating hazard, the narrow inlet was unsurpassed—golf balls headed for the water like iron pellets to a magnet. To get from tee to green, a foursome loaded their bags and four caddys into a scow, a rectangular vessel with high sides and duckboard flooring, and hauled it across the inlet with a rope and pulley.

The most heartbreaking hole of all was the seventeenth. Here players drove back across the inlet to a narrow fairway surrounded by marsh. It was a long hole with a hard dogleg to the right and the conservative golfers played it safe, across the inlet and a second shot parallel to the marsh. The more expert, or daring ones, drove diagonally across the inlet and the marsh to reach the green in one shot, about 250 yards. The drive had to be absolutely perfect, too short or to the right or left and the players were in the marsh. Too far and they were in an impossible mixture of bayberry bushes, blackberry vines and beach grass. The winds, always blowing in this area, and notoriously variable, added to the golfer's challenges.

Mr. Shaw found father to be the hardest working and the most trustworthy of his laborers and so made him the caretaker. The two men, the affluent, Harvard graduate, Boston socialite, and the high school dropout, Jack-of-all trades, worked closely together for 20 years. Father had a free hand in managing the six-man crew and the accounts. The two conferred as respected colleagues on technical details of the course—there were never strong disagreements or sharp words. Mr. Shaw trusted his manager totally and in return father was on call all the time and agonized over the monthly bills to make sure that every penny was justified.

Our house was only a half-mile away from the clubhouse so we saw a lot of Mr. Shaw and his guests. He chose not to have a clubhouse telephone and used our phone for all calls. Mr. Shaw and his guests always knocked, asked if they might use our phone, and thanked mother as they left. We retired to the kitchen, but left the door open to the dining room phone. The door was closed infrequently and, we suspected, only when Mr. Shaw's mistress was on the line. My brothers and I took incoming messages up to the "big house" and invariably were rewarded with a luscious piece of Belgian chocolate or the biggest and juiciest orange we had ever encountered.

From the middle of April until fall, groups of ten to 20 of Mr. Shaw's golfing friends were at Cedar Bank every weekend. Mrs. Shaw used the clubhouse for herself and female guests only once a year, the weekend prior to April 19th. Their only child, Quinny, Jr., didn't enjoy golf, preferring late fall duck hunting.

Golfing guests were serious about the game, playing four, 18-hole rounds on a weekend. Only a severe rainstorm would curtail this schedule. Visitors included Francis Ouimet, the first American amateur champion, Herbert Jacques, a two-time U.S. Golf Association President, and on one memorable occasion in 1931, the great Bobby Jones. His fluid, effortless swing was pure poetry. Wilbur caddied for him and was presented with the ball that Jones had used for the entire

From left, Quincy Adams Shaw, Francis Ouimet, Bobby Jones and Rodney Brown on the clubhouse deck, about 1933.

round. It was in perfect condition, no cuts or digs except for the imprint of his driver's face pattern in a few places.

Other frequent guests were C. Aubrey Smith, a Hollywood star of the 1930's and John Charles Thomas, a renowned concert tour tenor. Smith always played a "veddy" aristocratic, English gentleman in the movies and the sight of him playing a round with Mr. Shaw was awe-inspiring. The tenor's visits were exciting, not because of his golfing, but his singing plus an enormous zest for life. As soon as he returned to the clubhouse after a round, we could hear his voice, magnificent at first, and then turning sour when the group was well into the cocktail hour.

Thomas and his father-in-law often came on the golfing weekends together. They had formed a warm relationship based on mutual appreciation of the good life. Once a skunk had fallen into the hole housing our electric water pump when the two came to our house to use the phone. The pair must have just imbibed a cocktail or two because they insisted on

Caddies at Cedar Bank Links, about 1933. Back row, Bill Watson, Clyde "Monk" Wilson, Wilbur Sparrow, Bert Kelly, Donald Sparrow and George Rongner. Front row, Oliver, Aubrey Stott, Bob Pearson, Bob Watson, Fenton Sparrow, Nate Nickerson and Charlie Atwood.

helping mother with the problem. With a combination of ropes, planks and much laughter they got the skunk away from the house but both of them, and the house, were sprayed liberally with skunk juice.

Not one of us caddies played golf seriously and we weren't much help on details of the course or advising on the proper club. We were primarily golf bag toters and searchers for lost balls. The latter requirement was particularly important since the "rough" on Cedar Bank Links was heavy, wiry grass and beyond was an almost impenetrable thicket of vines, shrubs, weeds and tall grass. A willingness to roll up one's pant legs and go wading after a ball was also an important part of our job. Most of us accumulated a "set" of clubs, cast-offs from the players. One complained to me about his driver. "I've never hit a good shot with the damn thing, if this drive is no good, you can have it". His ball hooked badly and, without a word, he threw the club at me.

Herbert Jaques, an Eastham summer resident, practiced his driving on weekdays and hired me to stand down the fairway 200 yards or so to pick up the balls as they landed. I didn't dare admit that the path of the ball in flight was a total mystery to me and pretended to follow it, all the while terrified that it was going to hit me. The thud of the ball hitting the ground alerted me to the landing spot so I could run and pick it up. Mr. Jaques was such an excellent golfer that the ball always landed very near to me and I knew that my chances of being hit were high. Fortunately, there were lots of near misses but no hits.

Mr. Shaw celebrated Labor Day with the biggest party of the summer, an old-fashioned clambake—red hot rocks covered with seaweed, lobsters, steamers, corn and potatoes—all covered with a canvas tarp. The cocktail hour started when the pile was covered and continued as the tarp was removed and the meal served.

The parties were not open to local people, a fact which irritated one summer resident, a former Speaker of the Massachusetts House of Representatives. After being slighted a few times he devised a scheme to crash the party. Dressed only in a breech clout and tribal paint, he paddled over to the clambake site in a canoe and read a prepared announcement welcoming the White Man to these shores and assuring them of the peaceful intentions of the natives. Mr. Shaw and the guests were amused but not captivated and replied by throwing rocks and repelling the would-be party crasher.

Mr. Shaw came down to Cedar Bank less frequently after Labor Day. He had other places and other interests to fill out the rest of the year. In Eastham, he owned a gunning camp on Nauset Beach and a share of another on Great Pond. In Boston, he lived in his town house on Exeter Street and the family owned an estate on the North Shore called Pompeii's Gardens, said to live up to its name. To round out his year he stayed at his beach house on Nassau in the Bahamas for a few weeks in the winter and had rooms on permanent lease in hotels around New England.

After World War II, Mr. Shaw used the course less and less and finally abandoned it around 1950. Most of the property was sold to the federal government when the Cape Cod National Seashore was established in the area in 1959. The original clubhouse still stands and is kept in its pre-war condition by Shaw descendants, but Cedar Bank Links has returned to its pre-1925 condition. Only the outlines of the bunkers and an occasional grassy spot revealing the location of a green remain. The rest is overgrown with cedars, English oaks, scrub pine, bayberries, beach plum and hog cranberry.

GROWING UP ON CAPE COD

CHAPTER 10

TOUGHING OUT THE DEPRESSION

*T*he busiest parents in Eastham teach their
boys there's no such thing as a Depression.

Cape Codders didn't feel the rigor of the Great
Depression nearly as strongly as most of the rest of the nation.
The suffering was a lot more pronounced for city dwellers
than it was for those in rural areas such as Cape Cod, where
families could at least survive by fishing and farming.
Eastham's longterm population decrease slowed or even
stopped in the early 1930's because people were no longer
leaving to better themselves in the cities and also because of
what might be called Depression refugees. With no jobs
available in the cities, desperate families moved back to their
roots to seek help from relatives and friends.

Father helped one such family, the Warren Wilsons, by
providing a rental house next to our home and hiring Mr.
Wilson to work on his asparagus and turnip fields. His wife
knew the Sparrow family from her childhood days on the
Cape. The parents and their two young children moved to
Eastham from Camden, New Jersey, where Mr. Wilson had

been working for the Campbell Soup Company but had been let go when the economy collapsed after the Stock Market Crash of 1929. I welcomed the arrival of their son, Clyde, who was about my age. He and I became good friends when we found that we shared common interests—reading and complaining about our parents. He quickly acquired a nick-name, "Monk," given him by a classmate who thought his exuberant style of walking resembled that of a monkey. Clyde hated it but "Monk" stuck and I thought that he should have preferred it to either his first name or his second name, Earnest.

He and I spent a lot of time planning what we would do when we grew up. We agreed that we would not get trapped into mundane, nine-to-five jobs, and would travel to see the world. Once we swore a blood oath that when we had reached the advanced age of 30, we would take a year off and explore the upper reaches of the Amazon. When we actually did reach 30, both married and with young children, we met by chance and I reminded him of our naïve ambition. He thought me serious and felt obliged to point out the family commitments that would force him to decline the adventure.

Another of our neighbors got trapped in Eastham by the Depression. As Bud Cummings explained to me in an oral history interview, he was just out of college when he noticed the price of turnips in his Boston neighborhood grocery store. He calculated the yield of turnips per acre and concluded that he could become rich by growing turnips on several acres of family farmland in Eastham. He made the move in 1928. By the time he realized that his arithmetic had been faulty, the Depression was in full force and he and his wife Millie couldn't afford to go back to the city.

Bud and Millie were joined shortly by his half-brothers, Bob and Bill Watson, who had been orphaned in the very early 30's, and needed a place to live. They too, were roughly my age and were welcome additions to our Depression-enhanced gang of playmates.

The two Watson brothers were poles apart in looks and temperment. Both were slender and well-proportioned, but Bob, the older by two years, was blond and fair-skinned, while Bill had straight, dark brown hair and always looked middle-of-the-summer tanned. Bob was the extrovert with a hair-trigger temper. After a while, we learned to be cautious around him, partly because he wore a heavy gold ring on his left hand and didn't mind using that fist in a fight. Bill was more stable, serious, studious and slow to anger. In choosing up sides for any game, you usually selected Bill first.

Our family was not seriously inconvenienced by the Depression because father was such an outstanding provider. Whenever I become eloquent on the subject of our hardships, my children just ask me how we ate and then dissolve in gales of laughter as I tell them. In fact, we didn't suffer a bit in some ways, I've never eaten as well.

First of all, we had superb raw materials. Father kept chickens, cows and a pig, grew fruits and vegetables and went fishing and shellfishing. Wild animals and fowl such as deer or duck were never served; both parents thought that these meats had a gamey, strong flavor. For winter consumption, mother canned garden produce, made beach plum jelly, strawberry jam and put down eggs in water glass, (a sodium silicate solution which sealed the shells and preserved them for several months for cooking purposes). A professional butcher slaughtered and processed the summer-fattened pig in the fall to give us hams, bacon, pork, head cheese and sausage for winter use. Two or three barrels of apples were stored in the basement. If a natural disaster had confined us to the farm all winter long, we would have emerged in the spring happy and well fed.

Also, mother was an excellent cook, not the gourmet variety, but adept at good solid meat and potatoes and rich desserts. She stocked only a few spices: cinnamon, nutmeg and Bells sage for turkey stuffing. Dessert accompanied every meal: a real test of her willpower because she was diabetic, and sugars were forbidden. I remember the look of longing as we devoured the food she put before us.

She started a typical day by skimming the cream from three or four large, shallow pans of milk, which had rested in the pantry over night. The yield of cream was high; our Jersey cows gave an especially high butterfat content milk. Skimmed cream had to be ladled, it was too thick to pour. Skim milk was fed to the animals and surplus cream was converted to butter. We drank only whole, unpasteurized milk.

Breakfast was always a big meal, during asparagus season and off. Mother provided the same cholesterol-laden breakfasts on a year-round basis. She couldn't get away with a soup and sandwich lunch either. Father insisted on a substantial midday meal, always called dinner, and she had to have the meat, potatoes and dessert on the table promptly at noon. After school we had to have a snack such as a can of Campbell's tomato soup and buttered crackers. The weekday evening supper was less elaborate than dinner, but still a three-course, meat, potato and dessert meal.

Saturday night supper was special—always baked beans and brown bread. In the morning mother added molasses, brown sugar, a piece of salt pork, powdered mustard and an onion to parboiled, white pea beans in a brown crockery bean pot. The mixture baked all day in our wood-fired oven with occasional stirring and water added to keep the beans moist. Homemade, steamed brown bread, full of raisins, accompanied the beans. Now I would give my right arm for those authentic, homemade, baked beans. But I must be honest and admit that as a teenager, beans every Saturday night for more than ten years left me unenthused. Well, I suppose that the Czar's children might have tired of caviar.

Baked beans required the long, moderate, uniform heat supplied by our wood-fired kitchen stove. Another item which benefited from this type of heat was a pepper and onion dish which mother sometimes made on a Saturday. A large iron skillet filled with diced green peppers and Spanish onions sat on the back of the stove all day. Over a period of several hours, with frequent stirring, the mixture gradually slumped to a mushy dark brown sauce, filling the kitchen with a maddeningly wonderful aroma.

Sundays were the real heavy eating days. Breakfast might include leftover baked beans and cod fish cakes, quahog fritters with lots of ketchup or fried cornmeal mush with maple syrup. Dinner, delayed for an hour in recognition of the Sabbath, featured a roast joint or chicken. If available, the pepper onion sauce accompanied the roast. When cooking chicken (really an aged laying hen whose production had fallen below par), mother didn't brown the meat prior to stewing and so the gravy was bright yellow. The first time my wife served fricasseed chicken with a rich brown gravy, I advised her to ask mother how she managed to get that lovely, golden gravy. I quickly learned that golden yellow is vastly inferior to mahogany brown.

Thanksgiving dinner differed from the usual Sunday repast only by degree—more variety and more of everything. A huge, 20-pound turkey, of course, gravy with giblets, at least a half dozen vegetables including the famous white Eastham turnip and close to a limitless number of desserts—apple, mince, pumpkin and lemon sponge pies, chocolate pudding, coffee soufflé, steamed plum pudding and heavy cream to be ladled over every last one of them. In contrast to the conventional cold turkey sandwiches for supper, mother always served cold roast loin of pork at Thanksgiving supper to supplement the left over vegetables and desserts.

On Sunday evenings, mother finally got a break from the hot kitchen stove. Simple food was the rule, pilot crackers crumbled into milk or perhaps milk toast—buttered toast soaked in hot milk and topped with heavy cream.

Many of the everyday dishes mother served are still high on my list of all time gastronomic experiences—Cape Cod Turkey, asparagus on toast and fried eels to name a few. The basic ingredients of the first of these are salt cod and boiled potatoes, but every family had their own version of the final product. We mashed the potatoes and salt cod together on our plate and then poured fried salt pork scraps, hot fat and all, over the mixture. Others put the salt cod and sliced hard-boiled eggs in a cream sauce and combined this with the potatoes and pork scraps. Still another variation was boiled beets and onions mashed in with the potato. The dish varies from home to home and is really the Cape Cod equivalent of hash.

Asparagus to us meant only the tips which had broken off the stems during bunching. They were briefly steamed, placed on buttered toast, doused with heavy cream and seasoned with salt and pepper…. Heaven.

Freshly caught eels were another favorite. To catch eels, father chopped a hole in the ice covering Salt Pond and probed the muddy bottom with an eight-pronged eel spear on a 15- to 20-foot wooden pole. A violent vibration signaled that the prongs had encountered an eel. The skinned and cleaned eels were cut into small segments, dipped in coarse corn meal, and fried in hot bacon fat. Mother didn't relish preparing fried eels because the pieces twitched and jumped about as they fried. We couldn't get enough of the golden pieces of firm but tender flesh, delicately flavored with just a hint of fishiness.

In the winter when the kitchen was cool, Saturday morning was doughnut-making time. Mother had to keep shooing us away as we grabbed for the hot doughnut holes, smelling of cinnamon and nutmeg. Other memorable dishes were clam chowder, (no thickening please), steamers about two hours out of the bay, quahog pie, fried herring roe and countless others.

The thick, pale yellow cream mother served made every dessert extra special. We spooned it onto strawberry or blackberry or apple pie, hot gingerbread, coffee soufflé, even on boiled rice.

One of my friends inquired about my cholesterol count when I told him about the cream and all the other rich foods we ate. Mine is still low, perhaps because I inherited a resistance to such problems from a trencherman ancestor, Obed Sparrow. This early 18th century poem describes his enthusiasm for home cooking.

> *"And foremost in the battle's van*
> *Bold Obed leads his crew;*
> *He's always there his part to share,*
> *In deeds of derring do!*
> *And when he brings his prize to port,*
> *Thro' storm and flying foam;*
> *He'll proudly tell he'd conquer hell,*
> *On the grub he gets at home!"**

---

* According to Donald Trayser (Eastham, Massachusettss 1651-1951, the Eastham Tercentenary Committee, Eastham, Massachusetts), taken from a toast by the rhyming blacksmith, Peter Walker, in Eastham's Crosby Tavern in the 1800's.

CHAPTER 11

DOCTORS, DENTISTS AND A SULPHUR BAG

n which a doctor actually makes house calls, the four boys are subjected to treatment by a deaf dentist and home remedies such as a dose of sulfur and molasses, a camphor bag around the neck and skunk grease for a chest cold.

The old joke, "What does a doctor take for a cold? Answer, seven days", is as valid today as ever. Our mother, like most mothers, had many ways of dealing with the affliction and they were just as effective, or ineffective, as present-day treatments. First, she used a number of preventative measures designed to "build us up" so that we could better resist cold bugs. A favorite was Father John's Medicine, a pleasant-smelling, smooth, sweetish, patented concoction, which she considered a potent child builder-upper. It tasted great and, I'm sure, did us no harm. Once in a while, she tried to switch us to cod liver oil, but we fought the greasy, fishy, viscous, revolting stuff so vigorously, she always reverted to the wonderful Father John's.

In early fall, she made us put on our union suits and tied a walnut-sized bag of sulfur around our necks. Both under-

wear and sulfur remained until spring, although we did enjoy a weekly change of long under-wear after the Saturday night bath. Sulfur was supposed to ward off all disease-causing bacteria. To us it simply emitted a faint but unmistakable odor of rotten eggs and exposed us to ridicule from our friends who were not similarly equipped.

As soon as one of us was unlucky enough to catch cold, camphor replaced the sulfur. This waxy, white solid had a penetrating odor reminiscent of mixed turpentine and gasoline. Mother believed the pungent, nose-clearing, aromatic substance was a specific against cold bugs. The new cold fighter made us even more noticeable at school.

We only had to cough or sneeze once to be asked, "Are you catching a cold?" The remedies were just as unpleasant as the cold, and so we always denied being ill. But after the second sneeze, we were wrapped in blankets, placed next to the wood-fired kitchen range, and force-fed hot ginger tea, as close to the boiling point as possible. We sweated bullets as the combination of fiery ginger tea and cherry-red range top went to work. At this favorable reaction, mother rushed us upstairs to our unheated bedroom and into a pre-heated bed. A flannel-wrapped heated brick had been placed under the covers and moved about to warm the icy sheets. We grateful-ly curled around the brick, luxuriating in its residual warmth.

The following day mother would be after us to eat some

chicken soup. Our old, laying hen soup chickens were tough and a heavy layer of yellow fat floated on the broth. As today, nothing really shortened the course of the cold, and inevitably, it settled into our chests. This called for liberal applications of a cursed patent medicine, Musterole, which burned our chests and brought tears to our smarting eyes. In the neighboring Escobar family, skunk grease was used instead of Musterole, and how we envied those lucky Escobar kids.

Swollen glands accompanied the chest congestion and my mother's cure for this was Iodex rubbed lavishly over the throat and neck. This evil looking black ointment was relatively odorless and non-irritating, but the continued application left our necks with a dirty pallor, as though we hadn't seen a washcloth for months.

According to a recent Consumer Union publication, the effective ingredients in most of today's cough medicines are sugar and alcohol. Mother was well ahead of her time. When her cold reached the chest stage, she added a good dollop of whiskey to some honey, and kept the mixture warm on the back of the stove in an enameled tin cup. She was a strict teetotaler and always refused a social drink. Adamant on the subject, she even frowned on us boys having Coca Cola or other "tonics" because, "It taught us to drink from the bottle". Nevertheless, a chest cold called for heroic measures, and she partook freely of the contents of the tin cup. It seemed to do her a lot of good too.

Dr. Bell was called if the cold "hung on". His office was in Wellfleet, but he made daily rounds and so could be counted on to call at the house. The doctor, a tall, portly gentleman with thinning, gray hair, rimless spectacles and a "turkey wattle" neck, drove a recent vintage, black, Model T touring car. The very presence of the serious, confident Dr. Bell was reassuring. His imposing and mysterious large black bag opened like a mechanic's tool kit with flights of trays exhibiting row-on-row of vials filled with multi-colored pills and liquids. Exotic and vaguely alarming aromas floated from the opened black bag—it was a miniature drug store.

His examinations were thorough and gentle and his prescriptions, for colds at least, not at all hard to take—stay home from school a few days, keep warm, rest, (i.e., no chores) and take "spirits of nitre", a pleasant tasting, alcohol/ water solution of potassium nitrate. We were glad to see him and to follow his advice.

Not only did Dr. Bell bring along his own little drug store, he was also prepared to set broken bones, deliver babies, sew up cuts and perform tonsillectomies, or even appendectomies —at home. He removed Robert's tonsils in our family living room, with Robert fastened into the big rocking chair while his three brothers were outside, glued to the window.

I suspect that Dr. Bell had not taken refresher courses in medicine since his school days and probably didn't make a

practice of reading the medical journals. He was wonderful with the everyday medical problems, but missed badly with the origin of father's headaches. For at least ten years he treated a sinus condition and didn't even consider another source. As we learned in 1941, a benign tumor had been invading the frontal lobe of father's brain and causing excruciating pain. An early diagnosis could have saved years of suffering and mental deterioration.

In the days before vaccines and antibiotics, even doctors were helpless in the face of childhood diseases such as whooping cough, scarlet fever, measles, diphtheria and infantile paralysis. All they could do was to supply lots of tender, loving care, and this is what Dr. Bell did. When Robert was ill with diphtheria, we saw Dr. Bell at least once a day during a very difficult two-week period, and I'm convinced that the presence of this confident, caring doctor was important to Robert's recovery.

Every family had its own home remedies to deal with routine problems; we saved Dr. Bell for really serious situations. Deeply imbedded splinters were treated with drawing salve, a sticky liquid when hot, which solidified when poured onto the impacted area. After two or three days, the salve was yanked off, and the splinter came with it. Infected cuts and abrasions were soaked in Sulfo-Napthol, a patented germicide, which formed a milky white suspension in hot water and smelled strongly of coal tar. The active ingredient, sulfonated naptha, is now a suspected carcinogenic agent and definitely not a good thing to put on bare skin. Mustard plasters, sticky mixtures of powdered mustard and hot water spread on flannel cloth, and hot flaxseed poultices, the hotter the better, were other weapons in mother's home medicine chest.

In late spring, we were allowed to discard the bag of sulfur or camphor and change to summer underwear. This meant cutting the union suit off at the knees and elbows to provide a one-week period for the body to adjust before donning the summer garb. The underwear shearing became a first of May ceremony, marking the official end of winter. At the same time, we were administered a single, massive dose of sulfur and molasses—to thin the blood. I never understood what the mixture was supposed to accomplish, but imagined my slushy, oatmealy, winter blood thinning to a thin red fluid and racing through my veins like a spring flood.

When we developed an aching tooth, mother called one of two dentists; Dr. Radin or Dr. Bessie. The latter had started as a medical doctor but he shifted to dentistry when his hearing became so bad he had trouble interpreting the patient's vital signs. Dr. Bessie filled my first aching tooth, using a foot-powered drill. As he pumped away with left foot and applied the slow moving drill, wisps of steam came from my mouth and I screamed as loud as I could. He sensed something was wrong and inquired, "Does it hurt, does it hurt?" I yelled, "Es, es!" He nodded pleasantly and kept right on grinding.

We quickly persuaded our parents to send us to Dr. Radin whose hearing was perfect. Unfortunately, he preferred a quick fix for aching teeth – pulling them. I lost one or two teeth, which could have been saved with a simple filling.

Nobody of sound mind would wish to return to state-of-the-art 1930's medical or dental care. However, I sometimes think fondly of those days when subjected to a barrage of television blurbs for decongestants or cough suppression agents, "Fast, FAST, FAST relief and so on, *ad nauseum*. But then, when I think of the sulfur or camphor bag, sulfur and molasses, hot ginger tea, greasy chicken soup, Musterole, Iodex and, especially, the foot-powered dental drill, I am not so sure.

CHAPTER 12

SHOPPING AT HOME

M other shops at home—the old fashioned way. Who needs *The Enquirer* and *The Star* when you've got George Wiley, Link Nickerson and Freddy Gill?

Not only did Doctors make house calls, but merchants and tradesmen came to our house on a routine basis. Our fish peddler, Scurry Jack from Provincetown, was Portuguese, a short, Cape Verdean with a dark, wrinkled, weather-beaten face who always wore a battered fedora hat, blue denim overalls and a rubberized apron. The nickname came from his practice of scurrying about the Provincetown docks and fishing boats every day, as he sought the best deal on fish. His purchases were loaded into a gray box, half filled with crushed ice, and mounted on the back of a Model T. The only other equipment his mobile fish market required was a butcher block on the tail gate, a set of scales dangling from an outside hook, a wooden scabbard holding several lethal-looking knives, and a waste bucket hanging from the underside of the box.

Once a week, the Model T came jouncing into our driveway, the scales and bucket swinging wildly. Everything was absolutely fresh and top quality—swordfish, cod, flounder, haddock, halibut and mackerel. He didn't carry salmon, pollack or tautog. In those days, the former was considered a luxury and the latter both trash fish. Swordfish was all white or pinkish white with no dark meat. My mother thought that even a small streak of dark made the meat too strong, too "fishy" and fit only for cat food. Recently, I tried to buy all-white-meat swordfish at a local shop and was told flatly that, "It doesn't come that way." Well, it used to.

George Wiley, who worked for a general store in Wellfleet called Horton and Gill, delivered canned goods, packaged foods and kitchen staples such as sugar, flour and rice. A tall, mustached man with a twinkle in his eye, he possessed an inexhaustible supply of funny stories and gossip. He stuck with a horse and buggy long after everyone else had shifted to an automobile. One day he finally surrendered to modern technology, took driving lessons and bought a car. The lessons must have evaporated the first time he tried to drive into his garage, because he was heard yelling at the top of his lungs, "Whoa, Whoa, Whoa!" as the auto tore right through the back of the building.

George usually entered our house with an empty pipe in his mouth. My mother would take the hint and offer some of my father's pipe tobacco or one of his cigarettes. Carefully packing the pipe, (tearing the paper from the cigarette if that was the only tobacco available), he then put the pipe in his pocket, unlit. He repeated the performance at every house with a smoker and emptied the pipe into a can stashed in the grocery wagon.

At some point, Freddie Gill took over the grocery cart deliveries from George, but there was no let down in the flow of small talk. He was a large man with an expansive middle and a giant appetite for life. The only time he refused a drink was when, "I couldn't hear the question". We could count on him for the latest and most entertaining stories of the interesting happenings about town.

The butcher wagon proprietor, Byron Holmes, was another over-achiever like my father. Not only did he run a meat market in Orleans and operate the home delivery service, but he also played violin in an orchestra, which performed at many of the local dances and served as special policeman in Orleans. He was on call for almost every public event, as either violinist or traffic cop.

Link Nickerson carried the Watkins line of patent medicines and cooking aids such as baking powder and spices. Everyone called him Link because he was six feet six inches tall, weighed about 150 pounds, and when he sat down, seemed to fold up like the sections of a carpenter's rule. My mother especially looked forward to his weekly visits because he had a knack for collecting the juiciest gossip and a flair for spelling it out in vivid detail.

The iceman, Tom Brown, came to our house every three days during the hot summer months. He picked up a block of ice in his tongs, weighed it, carried it to the icebox on a leather pad slung over his back and then cut the block down until it fell into the available space. We were a bit in awe of him because he looked like a pirate boarding a captive ship as he entered the house: wiry but heavily muscled with a deep tan and an ice pick held between his drawn-back lips, a gold-filled tooth gleaming behind the ice pick. Despite our apprehensions, we couldn't resist hanging around during this operation to grab at the shower of cold slivers of ice as he reduced the block to the proper size in a few seconds.

Every three months, Mr. Malchman drove down from Hyannis to present his selection of dungarees, work shirts, Keds sneakers and other articles of apparel. His wares were displayed in a huge, bright green, wooden box on a Model T with foot-high gilt letters spelling out his name. The box so weighted down the tired Ford, that he had to turn around and back up any slope with a grade in excess of three percent—reverse gear was much more powerful than the forward speeds. Mr. Malchman was all business, no small talk or gossip from him, but he was one of the few Democrats on Cape Cod and our Republican mother always got into spirited political discussions with him.

Most of the merchants had time to stop and chat and had a rich supply of news, rumor and gossip. As in any small town, keeping a secret was not easy and distinguishing between fact, unsupported rumor and fiction, equally difficult. Since they called on most of the housewives of the outer Cape, their abundant store of information, or misinformation, was continually renewed. A hot item one fall was speculation on the identity of the man whose amorous activities were the basis for a best-selling novel about the torrid romance between a summer visitor and a Cape Codder. There was hardly a male in the right age group who escaped the scrutiny of merchants and housewives alike.

At another time, a businessman was sued for alienation of affections, charged by an aggrieved husband that the boss-secretary relationship was far from professional. The merchants and housewives discussed the case in exhaustive detail and a sense of righteous indignation.

Today's supermarkets don't offer the same opportunity for dissemination and enrichment of gossip. Weekly tabloids like *The Enquirer* and *The Star* lamely try to fulfill this need, but their gossip is about national or international figures. I sneak a peak and chuckle as I read of Marilyn Monroe's love affair with Albert Einstein or the 70-year-old woman giving birth to triplets. They are amusing, but I long for the far more interesting and immediate overheard stories of Eastham's carryings-on—the shenanigans of real live people who I knew and saw frequently. Those stories were gospel to my ears—after all, they came from unimpeachable sources: Byron Holmes, George Wiley, Freddy Gill and Link Nickerson.

CHAPTER 13

A CAPE COD SEA CAPTAIN

 ne Eastham native, the author's uncle, escapes from Cape Cod, captains ocean going vessels, survives a U-boat torpedo attack, lives on the west coast of Africa for several years, promoting trade between that area and the United States, and finally returns home to Eastham to retire

Father dropped out of school to help his mother with the family, but also to allow his younger brother, Robert, to finish high school and to attend the Massachusetts Nautical Training School—the forerunner of the present-day Massachusetts Maritime Academy. Captain Robert Weller Sparrow, or Uncle Rob, as he was known to his worshipful nephews, led a life that many Cape Cod boys only dreamed of. In 1910, after graduating at age 18 from the two-year training ship program, he served as junior

Cadet Robert Sparrow, seated on right, at the Massachusetts Nautical Training School.

officer for a few years on coastal ships and then went "deep water," which provided the opportunity to travel to ports all over the world. A contributing factor in this decision was the food supplied on the coastal vessels—in Uncle Rob's words, "monotonous beef and biscuits with weevils in the biscuits and worms in the beef".

After the United States entered the first World War, the *Columbian*, on which he was second officer, was chartered to a French company and fitted to carry horses. The ship's vets had been promised a bonus if no more than 150 horses died on the voyage. They encountered heavy seas and the horses fared poorly. After the first 150 died, the vets quit and the task of throwing the many dead horses overboard was left to the ship's crew.

On the return voyage, two days out of St. Naziare, the *Columbian* was stopped by a German U-Boat, torpedoed, and sunk after the crew had been transferred to small boats. They had to row for seven hours to reach the mainland. Within a year, Uncle Rob was made captain on his next ship, the *Dakotan*.

After the war he was put in charge of the African west coast operations of a joint venture between the U.S. Shipping Board and his employer, a steamship line, the Bull Company. He assumed responsibility for a fleet of 16 ships, working out of 57 ports stretching from the Canary Islands, along the African west coast to Angola. Exotic timbers, ivory, hides, gold, cocoa, aluminum and manganese ores were among the products shipped from these ports.

Uncle Rob was stationed in the Nigerian city of Lagos for four years from 1922 to 1926. At that time, Lagos was a primitive, small town—swampy, hot, humid and with limited 20th century amenities. His office had a dirt floor and he kept a revolver in the desk drawer to shoot at rats as they scurried across the floor. He was a frequent victim of malaria, endemic in the fetid climate, and wasn't unhappy when the federal government sold its portion of the fleet and he moved to New York to be the Barber Steamship Lines Marine Superintendent.

Now that he was based in New York and still unmarried, we saw a lot more of our uncle than in his African days. Father was especially glad to see him during the Prohibition years; Uncle Rob had no problem in getting the best liquors off the boats, and his bags always held a bottle of Johnny Walker Black Label Scotch. He never forgot that his big brother had left school so that he could get an education. Sometime during each of his visits he would write a check for father and insist he take the money. These sessions ended with torn checks littering the table and moist eyes all around.

Over the years, Uncle Rob acquired several pieces of real estate in Eastham and ended up with a 14-acre plot overlooking the Nauset Marshes. When he retired at age 69, he moved here with his bride, a longtime friend, Miss Eva Davies. A native of the Isle of Guernsey and a World War I Red Cross nurse, she had emigrated to New York after the war to work as head operating room nurse in a number of the city's hospitals. He had courted her ever since his West African days, but she was determinedly self-sufficient. Once he called to say he was taking the subway to call on her. Her reply to that was, "Save your nickel."

She accompanied him on some of his Eastham visits in the days before they were married, but was received coolly by his Cape Cod relatives. They misunderstood the relationship and thought she regarded him as a good catch and was pushing for marriage. The opposite was true, but their attitude generated lasting bad feelings on both sides.

In the late 1920's when our uncle started to ask Eva to be with him during his Eastham visits, father began to develop blinding headaches, which Dr. Bell treated as a sinus problem. The headaches continued in spite of Dr. Bell's ministrations. As a trained nurse, Eva voiced her concerns but was ignored as a troublemaker. She confided in me many years later that once, in 1928, when father was 40 years old, she found him sitting in the barn, holding his head and crying repeatedly, "Oh my God, oh my God." She said to our uncle, "I think that Dan may have a brain tumor." She was right, but it took many pain filled years for the condition to be discovered.

Uncle Rob moved to Boston in the 1960's and Eva finally accepted his proposal. After a few years in a Boston apartment, they moved to Eastham. In retirement, Rob and Eva built a house on the 14 acres and he spent a number of years eradicating the poison ivy, bayberry bush, locust and other pucker bush covering the property. The improved property had two asparagus beds and a vegetable garden. Asparagus was his specialty, and every morning during the growing season, he gave the biggest and most tender stalks to his friends.

Uncle Rob in one of his asparagus beds, about 1965.

Uncle Rob's corn field was plagued by worms chewing up the ears of corn. Nothing seemed to prevent the loss of the corn crop and he was ready to experiment with any suggested schemes. Learning that the worms hatched from larva that ladybugs particularly enjoyed, he sent to California for a quart of refrigerated bugs, warmed them and released them in his corn patch. The swarm hovered over the corn for a few minutes and then took off, en masse, for parts unknown, leaving him cursing and shaking his fist. We were going to try a tobacco cloth shroud the next year, but he died just as the corn stalks started to develop ears.

Some parts of Uncle Rob's retirement activities are difficult to document, especially his many kindnesses to friends and townspeople. My own two sons got to know him in the 1960's when they were in their late teens. The long hair, long beards and casual attire fad was at its height, and both boys were as hairy and casual as any of their peers. I am certain that Uncle Bob's spit and polish, maritime background, must have made him detest their appearance. Yet, he invited them to his home, took them for long walks, and gave them his full support with their teenage problems. That he was able to accept their lifestyle and took the time to try to help them provides clues as to the kind of man he was.

CHAPTER 14

MOXIE AND OTHER PETS

 very lazy pony named Moxie, a monkey with an appetite for grasshoppers and a colorful parrot with an unusual trick all make their separate appearances at our farm.

Uncle Rob was full of stories about the menageries he saw on the docks. We were wild with excitement when he asked if he should get us a baby elephant that a sailor had brought home. We made elaborate plans as to where we would keep him, what we would feed the baby, (pablum, bananas, milk?), and gleefully speculated on the astonished looks on our classmates' faces when we rode our elephant to school. We asked all fall about our newest pet, but he never arrived. I'm sure our folks killed the idea.

Monkeys were another readily available item on the New York docks, and the next summer, Uncle Rob asked if we would like one. Of course we would, but we didn't get our hopes quite as high as we had for the elephant. We had forgotten the offer, when the four of us came home from school one November day and found our stunned and despairing parents sitting in the kitchen, all doors and windows closed, observing a small, Capuchin monkey hopping from the table to the sink to the back of the stove and to the table again.

Our new pet, Jocko, did not become mother's favorite. He spent the winter months huddled in a blanket-covered cage next to the kitchen stove and the expression, "smells like a monkey's cage," took on a richer meaning for us. Robert made a little cage on wheels for his bicycle and took him to school a number of times, where he was always the hit of the day, if he stayed outside. We never succeeded in taming Jocko. Outside without a leash he was off like a shot into the woods or the barn, and when we found him, he tried to bite a piece out of our fingers.

His eating habits were unusual, in that he gobbled his food and stuffed any excess into cheek pouches. A banana disappeared in seconds and the pouches bulged as though he had the mumps. He enjoyed a walk in fields with long grass because he was fond of grasshoppers and quite adept at snatching them in mid-air as they jumped from stalk to stalk. In short order his pouches were stuffed with jumping, squirming insects.

As we grew accustomed to his presence, we became careless about keeping him on the leash and spent anxious hours searching the pine trees or the haymow. We were secretly pleased when mother found another home for him in Provincetown. The new family wasn't any more successful in domesticating him. He escaped, hid in the cold storage plant, and his frozen corpse was discovered months later.

After one especially good asparagus season, the four of us were given every boy's dream pet, a pony. Along with Moxie came a saddle, two-wheeled cart, four-wheeled surrey and assorted harness accessories. When father brought her home in his Brockway truck, we couldn't wait to get her saddled up and go for a gallop. The name implied that we were getting a lively prancing steed. Would we be able to control her? Wilbur, the oldest and biggest of the four of us, got the first ride. As he climbed into the saddle she turned her head, gave him a baleful look, and then took a hard nip at his leg. This seemed to be a promising start, a high-spirited beast who didn't like to be ridden. Well, we'd show her. Wilbur yanked her head around and applied the whip to let her know who was boss. She lowered her head and nibbled at the grass, ignoring repeated lashings. Finally, Wilbur gave up and we decided that she really deserved a few hours of rest to get acclimated to her new surroundings.

Rest, food, kindness, the whip: nothing worked. We would fight bitterly to get her a few hundred yards from her stall and then as soon as we turned her around, she broke for the barn in a hard trot. Moxie was a lazy, disagreeable equine, more interested in oats and her stall than work. We struggled with her for a few years and then, after Fenton broke a shoulder blade when she bucked and threw him to the ground, father unloaded her on a Chatham family with several boys and no experience with Shetland ponies.

Moxie with Wilbur holding the reins. Cousin Barbara Sibley and Fenton standing in the back, Mary Durlam and cousin Anna Harding seated and Donald standing in front.

Mother tolerated Moxie because we couldn't bring her in the house. We managed to keep pets given to us by Uncle Rob because she couldn't refuse them. In addition to animals, the sailors often brought back birds from Africa and tried to sell them on the New York docks. One year, he gave us a brilliantly plumed gray parrot, replete with green and blue tail feathers. These were Prohibition times and Uncle Rob had the usual bottle of Johnny Walker Black Label Whiskey in his luggage so the parrot had to be named Johnny Walker. He had one engaging trick, which involved making a loud cork-popping sound and then a drawn out gurgle-gurgle-gurgle whenever he was shown a bottle of whiskey. We marveled that Uncle Rob had been so lucky as to find a parrot with this name and this trick. Later he confessed that he had named the bird himself and spent many hours in his Brooklyn apartment training Johnny Walker in this trick as a joke for my father. We kept J.W. for a couple of years before Aunt Annie admired him and got him as a present from my mother, on the spot.

A third house pet that mother allowed, but only after hours of pleading, was a baby chipmunk that Fenton had found and kept until it was fully grown. "Chippy" was quite tame and enjoyed riding about on his shoulder. A squirrel-cage treadmill from a coffee can with cleats on the inside was the little chipmunk's favorite toy. He ran himself ragged, spinning the can until the lettering was just a blur. Fenton often took it to school in his pocket, without our mother's knowledge, and played with it when school work bored him. Chippy disappeared that spring, answering the irresistible lure of a female chipmunk, we guessed.

CHAPTER 15

THE LITTLE YELLOW SCHOOLHOUSE

*T*he four Sparrow brothers attend classes and make mischief, as did generations of their ancestors.

Not many people, I suspect, can point to a museum as their old schoolhouse. I'll admit to a sense of pride as I drive past the Eastham Historical Society's one-room schoolhouse museum on Nauset Road. It's too bad more of its graduates didn't seek public office—what great campaign material!

The museum building started as a one-room schoolhouse in 1879, expanded to three rooms in 1905, and then after the school closed in 1936, the original room was restored to house the museum. When I was a student, the three-room structure was painted a bright yellow as now, and had identical wings, each with two entranceways leading to a small coatroom and then into a 24-by-30-foot main room. Boys were never allowed to use the girl's entry and vice versa. Even now, I have a slightly uneasy feeling when visiting the Museum via the (former) girl's entrance.

Classrooms were equipped with 20 to 30 wooden lid-top desks, each with an attached seat and iron grillwork legs

Eastham Grammar School, about 1910. The surviving wing, in front, now houses the Eastham Historical Society Museum.

screwed to the floor. A large pot-bellied stove provided wintertime heat. There was no electricity and no lamps, school was open only during the day. Toilet facilities were the old fashioned kind in an outhouse in back of the school building.

The first grade teacher, Miss Florence Keith, had been there for many years. She bore a striking resemblance to Eleanor Roosevelt—close to six feet tall, protruding front teeth with an ever-present, warm, lovely smile. She was our neighbor on Nauset Road and I spent a lot of pre-first grade time helping her in her garden. Painlessly, I got the equivalent of first grade training before I was six. In addition, mother had been a teacher before her marriage, and taught me to read and write prior to school. With this preparation, Miss Keith was able to double promote me to the third grade in June.

After zooming through Miss Keith's room, I spent three comfortable years with Mrs. Virginia Horton, a kind, motherly, undemanding lady, short and plump with a cheery round face. Her long, heavy, dark brown hair was fashioned into a tight-fitting helmet, gathered into a bun at the back. The bun served as a storage place for pencils and the three or four that were always sticking out, Indian headdress style, gave her a rather jaunty look.

Classes were small, not more than 20 students in each of the three classrooms, and so we received lots of individual attention. We were pretty much on our own during recess and lunch breaks; there was no organized play or sports. We gobbled lunch at our desks and then rushed outside to scuffle in the sandy, dusty soil or play tag, prisoner's base, hilly-hi-over, Rover Red Rover and other schoolyard games. All eight grades used the same yard, but there was little overlap in the play. We understood that students from each of the three classrooms didn't stray too far from their entry.

Once a week, music and art teachers visited each of the schools in the outer Cape district. Musical education received a lot of attention. A Mr. Thomas Nasi had just been hired as Director of Musical Education for the Outer Cape school systems, and everyone had to play a musical instrument. A snare drum in the Eastham Drum and Bugle Corps was the lot

Eastham Grammar School Drum and Bugle Corps Donald Sparrow on far right in back, Fenton third from left in front.

for tone deaf students such as I. Even that position was something of a trial for the teachers because I didn't bother to learn to read music and simply played along with the bugles carrying the melody.

Few of the would-be musicians, including my brother Fenton who played the bugle, were much more talented than I. Mr. Nasi tried to hide his anguish as we tootled and banged away during practice. Nevertheless, we were greatly pleased with ourselves on Memorial Day when we dressed up in our snappy uniforms, paraded along County Road (now Route 6) to Evergreen Cemetery and then rode the school bus to Orleans to march in its parade. These were the only two times each year we were allowed to play in public.

We walked the mile to and from school in all but the worst weather. A bad rain storm forced us to take the bus, a rickety conveyance outfitted with fabric curtains with little isinglass inserts, rolled up in good weather and unrolled in rain or cold. The windshield wiper was hand operated and in heavy rain the driver, Mr. Harry Collins, had to lean forward, peer intently through the rivulets of water, steer with one hand, and operate the wiper with the other.

From the sweet, gentle Mrs. Horton we went to Mr. Otto Nickerson, Grammar School Principal and teacher of grades six through eight. He was tall and slender with craggy, Lincolnesque features and a pompadour hairdo which accentuated his height. He had a reputation as a strict teacher who tolerated no nonsense. When a student seriously misbehaved, (throwing too many spitballs, for example), Mr. Nickerson brought him to the front of the room, took a wicked-looking leather strap from the desk drawer, asked the student to hold out a palm and administered one sharp whack. Almost every male student from those days claims that on the downswing, he snatched back his hand and Mr. Nickerson hit his own knee. Wilbur was the one in our family who received the treatment and claimed to have pulled off Mr. trick. The next stroke was unusually severe, he reported. Otto never used the strap on me and, in reality, he only needed to resort to it a few times a year, but the threat was always there.

Girls were spared the strap. However, on one occasion a sixth grader so irritated him that he took her over his knee and spanked her. Hearing about this unusual event, father commented, "It's a wonder he didn't burn his hand." I remember that we were all surprised that our classmate's naughty reputation had spread to the adult level.

I was lucky enough to meet with Mr. Otto again shortly before his death in 1992. When I commented that we had greatly feared triggering his wrath, he seemed pleased. He showed me the leather strap, a piece of harness measuring one foot long, one-and-one-half inches wide and one quarter inch thick. No wonder it was an effective deterrent. He had changed remarkably little since I graduated. His hair was white and perhaps he had put on a few pounds, but otherwise, he could have been standing before his desk, giving out tomorrow's arithmetic assignment, or reaching for "the strap."

In Mr. Nickerson's room, as in the other two, I listened to all the classes and so at the end of the sixth grade year, knew almost everything offered in all three grades. As a result I skipped the seventh grade and joined the 13- or 14-year-old eighth graders at the tender age of 11. Double promotions were common in those days. Fortunately, the practice has since been abandoned. Although able to handle the academic work, I was socially and emotionally quite immature and felt insecure associating with my older classmates.

Eighth grade was memorable because of two events unrelated to school: the Lindbergh baby kidnapping and the Hoover-Roosevelt Presidential race. Like the rest of the country, we were all intensely interested in the kidnapping story, a major topic of conversation in 1933. Charles Lindbergh was our greatest hero. Standard schoolboy attire was a leather aviator's helmet, leather jacket with knitted cuffs and a silk scarf knotted casually around the neck in imitation of the "Lone Eagle." His book about his transatlantic flight, *We* was a bestseller and anyone saying, "We are going to do this," inevitably got the response, "Where do you get that 'We' stuff?" We were devastated when we heard on the radio that the baby's body had been discovered.

The Depression had generated unusual interest in the Presidential election of 1933, even among us eighth graders. We couldn't help but hear the hour-long speeches as our parents clung to the Atwater Kent loudspeaker horn. Eastham was heavily Republican then, election returns typically showed 100 votes for the Republican candidate versus four for the Democrat and everyone in town knew precisely who those four misguided souls were. The straw poll in Mr. Nickerson's room predicted Hoover by a landslide; we mirrored the views of our parents, and the ill-fated *Literary Digest*.

In June, the eight members of the 1933 Grammar School graduating class paraded onto the stage of the town hall. The stage curtain, covered with local merchants' ads, now serves as a backdrop for the receptionist in today's town hall. The valedictorian was my best friend and fellow double promotion student, Monk Wilson. As salutatorian, I gave a serious speech on some unremembered subject but my first suit—a double breasted, blue serge with my first long pants—is still clear in my memory. Wilbur wore it first for his graduation in 1931 and then it was Robert's turn in 1932. Mother had to alter pants and jacket drastically to fit my smaller, (two years younger) frame. It hung on me like the suit on a scarecrow dummy.

Next fall we headed for Orleans High, a much larger school with over 100 pupils in four grades and 25 in the freshman class. Two of our classmates called it quits and the remaining six of us faced the fall with some trepidation, worrying about new classmates who had been together for eight years, bigger classes and, we feared, stiffer academic standards.

Donald Sparrow in graduation attire, a cut-down blue serge suit.

CHAPTER 16

THE BIGGEST BANG FOR THE BUCK

 n which uninhibited use of firecrackers was the norm and a few close calls were the result.

The Fourth of July was the most eagerly anticipated holiday of the year. School was out, the asparagus cutting season was ending, we had our summer pineapple clip and now we could give our undivided attention to the business of shooting off our fireworks.

Planning for our Fourth had actually started earlier in the spring when the catalogs arrived. There were no restrictions on the sale and use of fireworks, and the four of us spent hours poring through the catalogs, worrying about the quantities of torpedoes and sparklers we should buy, debating the merits of two-inch salutes versus cherry bombs, comparing the cost of the items with our carefully hoarded resources so as to get the "biggest bang for the buck." Each brother bought his own, personal arsenal; there was no pooling of resources. Younger boys with limited pocket money favored a mix: lady and monkey crackers mingled with an assortment of the inexpensive torpedoes and sparklers. Older boys equipped with a fatter wallet went for the heavy artillery: two inch salutes, cherry bombs and even a few larger noise makers.

Four- and even six-inch crackers were offered and the catalogs implied that these would yield a deafening blast second only to the explosion of Krakatoa's volcano. Once we took the plunge and ordered one of the six-incher's, but found it disappointing, not much noisier than the two-inch salutes—mostly just an imposing cardboard cylinder.

The first firecrackers started to go off at daybreak, and a steady drumfire of explosions continued through much of the

day. A glowing piece of punk, for lighting fuses, was with us at all times. It burned very slowly and gave off a pungent, unforgettable odor, which only reinforced our belief that it was made of dried, compressed cow chips.

Tiny lady crackers came in groups of 24 and usually were set off as a unit to achieve a satisfactory, machine gun chatter. But our workhorse was the monkey cracker. About one and a half inches long, it exploded with a satisfyingly loud bang and was quite cheap. To get the maximum effect, we held the lighted cracker as long as we dared, and then hurled it so that it exploded in mid-air. Sometimes, we misjudged, and by the end of the day, our fingers were covered with blood blisters and superficial burns. In addition, we were temporarily deaf.

Two-inch salutes and cherry bombs were bigger, more powerful and considerably more expensive than monkey crackers. We devoted much time and ingenuity to enhancing the impact of this portion of our war chest. Tossing them into a five-gallon milk can and replacing the cover was one way of raising the blast decibel level. We also taped a salute or bomb to a phonograph record with the fuse inserted through the center hole, ignited the fuse and scaled the record. If the timing was right, the explosion came in mid-air and scattered fragments of the brittle, shellac records all over the country-side. We discovered that cherry bomb fuses would remain lit even when thrown in water. The explosion, when we weight-ed them with lead strips, threw water, mud and sometimes even small fish, high into the air. Nothing was wasted. We broke duds in half and ignited the powder directly. It burned violently, spitting out a shower of bluish white sparks.

One dangerous trick, always conducted out of view of our folks, was a duel; with Roman candles. The two foot long cylinders shot a series of ten soft, luminous fireballs a dis-tance of 20 to 40 feet, at five-second intervals. They were intended to be aimed at the sky but we had more fun fighting duels at 20 paces. The slow moving fireballs were fairly easy to avoid, body hits were uncommon and contact with bare skin unusual, so we escaped without serious injury.

A gift from a misguided adult—a foot-long cannon and a can of black powder—once led to a minor disaster. Our par-ents were unaware of our treasure and we made sure that they didn't find out. Anxious to try it out, a gang of us took it to the field behind a neighbor's house, loaded it with a substan-tial charge of gunpowder, rammed this down with a wad of paper, and lit the fuse inserted into the touch hole. The gang ran for cover and waited eagerly, hands over ears, for the anticipated giant flash and bang. Time passed, nothing happened, and so Fenton cautiously crawled toward the cannon. Just as he got there and raised his head to inspect the fuse, the gun went off. The explosion blew grains of gunpowder back through the touch hole and directly into his face. He ran off across the fields in a panic, blood streaming from his face, with the gang trying to catch up to him. Finally able to wrestle him to the ground, we escorted him home and alerted our parents. Dr. Bell sent him to a specialist who managed to dig out most of the particles, some from his eyeballs. Father and mother spent considerable time over the next several weeks digging bits from his face. They were so grateful that there was no permanent damage, we got off with a light reprimand. Fenton still has a number of small, blue powder specks in his face as souvenirs of this close call.

By nightfall, we had exhausted the heavy artillery and finished with lighted sparklers and the remaining Roman candles. Mr. Shaw sometimes sent a box of pinwheels, sky rockets and other set pieces, but by twilight, we were a bit jaded and more interested in collecting the rice paper parachutes floating down with the remains of aerial bombs. Also, we felt let down, somewhat disappointed; our explosives hadn't been as spectacular as anticipated. We went to bed plotting next year's action. Maybe we ought to sink most of our money into a few, huge set pieces, or maybe…

I look back on those times with mixed emotions. It was great fun, but I am amazed that we all survived without major injury or burning down the farmhouse. As a parent and grandparent, I am pleased that the days of unlimited use of fireworks have been legislated out of existence.

CHAPTER 17

CAMPING OUT

$\mathcal{T}$he Sparrow boys and their friends live carefree, Huckleberry Finn summers.

Now that school was out, and Fourth of July behind us, we spent most of our free time near or on the water. This was easy since we had a pond in our back yard, and were within walking distance of many fresh and salt water ponds, as well as the salt marshes and the Atlantic Ocean. The first step up from our little, backyard body of water was Minister's Pond, bigger, deeper and only a mile away from home.

At the age of six, I learned to swim, or learned that I could swim, in Minister's Pond. "Dog paddling" in shallow water was second nature for some time, but going into deeper water was too scary until Wilbur and Robert gave me a ride in an ancient rowboat they had salvaged, "The Wreck of the Hesperus." We were 30 feet from shore when it slowly settled into the water and sank. I just dog-paddled to shore, to the approving applause of the older boys. After that, armed with the knowledge that I could swim, I joined the others in exploring the further reaches of Minister's Pond.

It was also called Spectacle Pond because a small spit of land divided it into two roughly circular areas. The peninsula was close to inaccessible from the land because of a prickly brier filled swamp at its base. Bob Watson had a bright red, canvas canoe and this enabled us to explore the spit of land. Nobody else used it and over the years, we came to think of it as our own private preserve, our favorite camp site. The gang, Bob and Bill Watson, Monk Wilson, Ken Mayo, Fenton and I, cleared away the underbrush, constructed a small dock and generally made ourselves right at home. Each of us had his own site with a pup tent, left in place for the summer, and equipped with bedding and even a flag pole with the Stars and Stripes flying when we were in residence.

We enjoyed a Huck Finn life, fishing, swimming, exploring the two ponds or just "hanging out" for several days at a time. When our food supply ran out we went home to replenish it. Our parents were hardly non-caring or overly permissive people, and it must have required unusual self-control to allow us to be away from home, unsupervised, for two or three days at a time.

Our meals were simple: hotdogs or hamburg cooked over an open campfire and canned fruits for dessert. Once, in an emergency, two of us ate a squirrel. A heavy rain had soaked us for several days, and the only thing in our food locker was a quarter pound of butter. As we sat in our pup tent, clothing wet and mildewed, hungry and trying to avoid the dripping water, a squirrel jumped onto the tent, then to a pine branch no more than ten feet away, and sat there chattering at us. We crawled out and hurled campfire rocks in the direction of the cocky little animal. To our great surprise and wild joy, one stone, a lucky hit, knocked him down. Armed with a Boy Scout knife, we skinned and dressed the animal and fried its hindquarters in the butter. It was absolutely delicious.

We fished Minister's Pond every day, but caught mostly smallish perch, sunfish, pickerel and an occasional hornpout —altogether a small, bony and muddy-tasting bunch. When we proudly brought our catch home, mother told us that the miserable little things were only good for fertilizer.

Our most exciting catch was a snapping turtle, two feet in diameter. We spotted it resting in about 15 feet of water and took turns dragging a baited hook past its nose. Finally, the turtle grabbed it and gave a tug—the opening round in what became an epic struggle. The 40 pounder dug in and couldn't be budged from the bottom of the pond without overturning the canoe. Only by paddling to shore and standing on firm ground, could we horse the beast into shallow water. Now he was fighting mad, (we decided it had to be a male), snapping savagely with razor sharp jaws and ripping with lethal-looking claws at anyone who came close. The five of us splashed about frantically in the water, avoiding tooth and claw while trying to figure out what to do with our prize. Bob tried to dispatch it with a hatchet, but succeeded only in chopping a rather large hole in his canoe. Fenton thrust a half inch stick at him and his teeth went through it as though it were butter. The stick-in-the-mouth approach finally worked, we gave him larger and larger sticks until he couldn't get through it. He was too stubborn to let go of a one inch pine bough. We wrapped several turns of fishing line around the stick and head, turned him over and managed to secure the claws with more line. Now we dared put him into a gunnysack and, gingerly, transported him to Uncle Dan's pond. Here we kept him alive for several days in a large chicken wire cage before selling him to Mr. Shaw, who had Boston's Somerset Club chef make him into soup.

We came close to getting into really serious trouble one night when we staged an impromptu raid on a tent colony on the other side of the pond. The brilliant idea struck us about midnight, inspired by the young girls we had seen among the vacationing families. Equipped with sticks and pans, whistles and even a bugle, we paddled silently across the pond, stole into the middle of the tents and let loose with our noisemakers. Giggling like fools, we made our escape before the unsuspecting campers knew what hit them.

Back at our own camp, we rehashed the adventure and decided it had been so much fun we should give a repeat performance. Unfortunately, the tent inhabitants were wide awake, hopping mad and ready for the chase. Several of us were captured. Bill Watson had the presence of mind to submerge in the pond and breath through a hollow reed until the searchers gave up. Bob Watson just outran them all, but he was wearing a pair of light tan pants and the campers reported to the police that some of us had been naked. We managed to clear up that misunderstanding and escaped with a light reprimand, if we promised to stay on our own side of the pond after dark.

When fresh water camping began to pale, we transferred operations to Nauset Beach on the Atlantic Ocean. Few cars were equipped to travel on the loose sand and so we could live pretty much as we pleased, if we camped on the dunes, a mile or so beyond the end of the paved road. To get there we loaded up our little skiff with its twelve horse outboard motor, (a gift from father after a good asparagus season), and motored through the Nauset Marshes to the dunes. We pitched pup tents in a circle about the campfire and, as at Minister's Pond, brought enough food to last for several days, supplemented with fresh fish and clams. Most evenings were capped with an enormous bonfire, the multi-colored flames leaping 20 or 30 feet into the air. It became a routine challenge to build a bigger fire than the previous evening and with the beach covered with driftwood, we had no problem in collecting enough to create an arsonist's delight every night. Once we found a bonanza, heavy timbers of an old wreck, which had emerged as the sand dunes shifted. The moist, rotting wood did not burn easily and we had to build gigantic fires against the huge beams to dry them out. It took us a whole summer, but the wreck was finally consumed. We may have destroyed a priceless relic by our innocent but regrettable action.

One summer, our camping group included a teenager who was an orphan living with a local family as a ward of the state. "Red" was an expert on the guitar and also had a magnificent voice. Every evening, in front of the roaring camp fire, he went through his rich and varied repertoire—popular songs such as "Red Sails in the Sunset," sentimental ballads, mildly risqué tunes like "The Foggy, Foggy Dew" or ribald ditties. I remember only the refrain of one of the latter—"A Diamond Ring, A Watch and a Chain and a Little Black Mustache".

The number of campers varied from time to time, but the composition of the group was totally male. As we entered our teens we began to lose the older ones, especially after a clear night with the moon's path of light stretching from shore to horizon across the ocean, the surge and roar of the waves in the background, and the glowing coals before us. Our thoughts were turning to other matters—the girl we had met on the beach that day, or a classmate who was away for the summer with her parents.

CHAPTER 18

QUAHOGGING FOR FUN AND PROFIT

*T*he teenage shellfish consortium suffers a disappointing summer.

In the Depression days of the early 1920's and 1930's, clams and quahogs were a major part of many Eastham diets—quahog chowder, quahog fritters, steamed clams, fried clams and quahog pie. We did eat a lot of shellfish, as did our ancestors and the earlier inhabitants of the outer Cape, the Nauset Indians. The first written account of the Nauset Marshes, recorded by Champlain when he and his men explored the area in 1605, mentions huge piles of shells next to the Indian dwellings which lined the shores.

For the uninitiated, to a Cape Codder the term "clam" refers to the soft-shelled steamer clam, which is so delicious when steamed and dipped in butter or dipped in batter and fried. "Quahog" refers to the hard-shelled clam, also known as "littleneck", "cherrystone", or "chowder", depending upon its size, and eaten raw on the half shell when small, or cut up for chowder when large.

Even at the beginning of the 20th century, it was still possible to take large quantities of clams and quahogs. Looking at a map of the area, Uncle Rob pointed out a hummock called Joe Mayo's Hook and said, "Oh yes, the Hook is the highest point around, I always saved that for last so I could top off my barrel of clams on the tide".

Clams were not nearly as plentiful for us as in Uncle Rob's day, and digging for clams or "scratching" quahogs was backbreaking work. Further, in the summer, when we had spare time, prices were at their lowest. A rounded, ten-quart bucket of littlenecks and cherrystones might bring 50 cents versus two dollars in late fall or winter when digging conditions were much less attractive. Price inflation generated, in part, by tourism was still many years away.

One summer, when the asparagus season was over and none of us had lined up worthwhile moneymaking projects, the four of us formed a quahog digging/marketing consortium. Our strategy was to go out every day, put the day's harvest into a selected spot at the water's edge, and then retrieve the shellfish in the fall or winter when prices recovered from the summer slump. A plus was the expected ingrowth while the quahogs were bedded down. Then, as now, it was possible to stake out a plot between high and low tide, post it and register it with the town authorities, (Such areas are now called grants and cover an acre or two). Nobody was supposed to dig within the posted area. Our staked area was divided into quadrants, one for each of the partners.

We rowed out on the falling tide that summer, every day at the start, and scratched for quahogs. It was hard work. Large areas of the Marsh had silted up considerably since my uncle's time, and we frequently got stuck on the flats. We spent a lot of time up to our knees, or beyond, pushing on our stranded rowboat in the slimy black muck that smelled strongly of decaying organic matter. Razor clams were another problem. They had a distressing tendency to die in a vertical position, with their surgical-steel-sharp shells one-half-inch apart and just barely visible. Working bare-footed we all nursed one or more pairs of parallel cuts on the edges of our feet throughout most of the summer.

Starting with great enthusiasm, we went out every day and carefully bedded down our harvest in the assigned area. Interest waned as the summer dragged along, but we thought we might have bedded two or three bushels each by Labor Day. That autumn was a long, warm one and we grew more impatient every day as we waited for cold weather, and an explosion in shellfish prices. Our imagined incremental growth became larger, and by November, we were confident that three bushels had grown to six. We learned that fall not to count our quahogs before, etc. Apparently, some unprincipled person had scratched in our posted region and none of us got back as much as we had deposited.

Hardy souls went clamming and quahogging in the winter in Salt Pond, the Marshes or the west shore (on Cape Cod Bay). I tried the latter location only once, one winter when weather conditions were just right. After a long, cold spell, ice floes had built up on the shore and as the tide moved the blocks of ice back and forth, the surface sand was scraped away, uncovering the quahogs. At low tide, all we had to do was climb over the ice and pick them up. Word got around quickly. We raced over to First Encounter Beach and made our way across the ice floes. The flats were covered with quahogs and we had no trouble in filling our bushel bags. Now, the really heavy work began. We had to lug the full burlap bags back to shore, over the ice cakes, slipping and sliding, falling into puddles of icy salt water, banging head and limbs. Several times I was on the point of abandoning my "easy" bushel of shellfish. Four bedraggled quahoggers finally made it to dry ground, cursing and vowing, "Never again."

Vacationing on the Cape in later years, I enjoyed going with Uncle Rob to the Marshes to dig clams. The man who "topped off his barrel on the tide" in his youth was still able, at age 75, to fill the allowed ten-quart bucket much more rapidly than I. He wore hip boots and got down on his knees, the better to work with his short handled clam digger. The air was full of sand and large piles of it grew quickly around his work area. We took our clams to Salt Pond to wash them and there ran into Phil Schwind, Eastham's shellfish warden. He was a gnarled, weatherbeaten commercial fisherman who posed as a town character, but in reality, was a skilled writer with a number of published books to his credit. Phil engaged my uncle in conversation as follows,

"Sorry to hear about your hoss."

"What's that?"

"Sorry to hear about your hoss."

"I don't understand, I don't have a horse."

"Well, I saw you digging that hole down there on the flats at Coast Guard Beach and thought you must be burying a hoss."

Digging for shellfish in Eastham's Salt Pond has become an extremely popular tourist event. The Town's natural resources department seeds the pond with baby quahogs, and then opens a portion of the shore on Sundays throughout the summer. Visitors armed with rakes, shovels, hoes and other assorted tools crowd the shores. Recently, our English daughter-in-law tried it. I tried to discourage her saying that I didn't like crowds, the place had been dug out. It was a waste of time and so on. Marilyn came back with a full ten-quart bucket, and I took a gentle but thorough, English-style ribbing until I learned that the young assistant shellfish warden had seen to it that she knew where he had thrown back the quahogs from heaped up or over the legal limit buckets. The eye-popping bathing suit Marilyn wore may have had something to do with the warden's generosity. Nevertheless, she got her bucket on the tide. Uncle Rob would have been proud of her.

CHAPTER 19

SPARE TIME PURSUITS

*T*he Sparrow boys find creative ways to make use of their spare time.

Ponds, ocean and beaches were an important part of our summer, but we spent a lot of time on land-based games also. Backyard baseball games in summer and touch football games in the fall were common, but we couldn't muster enough boys for a full complement of a baseball nine or a football eleven and it was difficult to sustain interest in the games. We had to use some creativity to avoid boredom in our spare time.

Bicycle polo was "in" one summer and we played it every day. Our mallet heads came from the family croquet set and handles were fashioned from the strong and whippy arrowwood shrub. An old baseball served as a polo ball. The bicycle polo craze lasted only part of one summer because tempers rose as the action got rougher, and it became tempting to take a shot at the opponent's bicycle, rather than the ball. As a result, our bikes needed increasingly frequent repairs and our parents put a stop to the carnage before one of us was injured, or our bank accounts were depleted by bills for repair parts from Sears Roebuck.

Another summer, pillow fighting on stilts was the rage. Contestants mounted on stilts and with one arm clamped around the pole tried to knock each other to the ground with a pillow. Good balance, agility, strength, and manual dexterity all were important in this demanding game. I have thought that it could become an Olympic event, certainly more exciting than sumo wrestling. A stoic acceptance of bruises and abrasions sustained when the loser hit the ground was also a desirable stilt-pillow fighting characteristic. This sport didn't last the summer either, too many medical emergencies.

Guns were another part of our everyday summer activities. Starting with cap guns, we graduated to BB guns, then to a 22-caliber rifle and, when we reached the age of 14 or so, a 12-gauge shotgun. There were no restrictions on the possession or use of guns. We ordered by mail from Sears and stored them casually in the back shed or the barn. Our folks drilled us on the proper use of the guns and we respected the rules. I can't remember a single accident or injury resulting from our use of the weapons.

We became reasonably good shots. A bunch of wild grapes hanging out of reach fell into our hands when we severed the stem with a BB. Hundreds of tin cans and bottles littered the bottom of Uncle Dan's Pond, sunk by BB's or 22 slugs. The Eastham dump was another place for shooting bottles, cans and sometimes rats. We took an occasional shot at frogs or birds. Seagulls were on the protected list, (as they are now), but I couldn't resist a shot now and then, always unsuccessfully. I was convinced that they were constructed with a three inch, bulletproof layer of feathers about a miniscule body. Many times, a sure shot resulted only in a haughty start from the arrogant creature as it flew off.

In winter, an abandoned chicken farm hatchery next to our house was the focal point of our playtime. Mr. Shaw owned the property and gave us permission to use the brooder house as a recreation area. With stored material pushed against the wall and hoops installed, we had our own private, miniature, (20- by 30-foot), basketball court. It was far from a perfect court; with hoops only six feet high and rafters seven feet from the floor, it made longer shots difficult. We learned to shoot from certain points on the floor and to arch the shots just right to avoid both the rafters and the roof. This "hall" was our gym for a few years, but all the scrimmaging didn't help most of us when we went out for the high school basketball team, we couldn't adjust to all that wide-open space.

Another winter sport, in addition to skating and hockey, was ping-pong. Again, we had to improvise a bit on equipment, using our family dining room table as a playing area. It was only two-third's the regulation size, with rounded edges and corners, and there was less than three feet between table and wall on three sides. This configuration favored a forcing, up-to-the-net type of game and quick reflexes to return the frequent bounces off rounded edges.

At age 13 I entered a WPA sponsored ping-pong tournament held in the basement of the Eastham Town Hall. The dining room arena had provided the right kind of training and I survived to the semi-finals, where my opponent was John Ullman, about 15 years older and much too good for me. He won handily, but I was so obviously chagrined that he volunteered to replay the match, best two out of three. The second time around gave the same result, but it took much of the sting out of the loss. He told me that he had also learned to play ping-pong on the family dining room table and so my style of play was very familiar to him. When reminded of his kindness 50 or so years later, the longtime managing editor of

The Cape Codder vigorously denied that it ever happened. Perhaps he doesn't want to damage his crusty old curmudgeon image.

One year my Christmas present was a mold for making three lead figures—an Indian and two cowboys on horseback. Our basement furnace served as a forge, (vented, which probably saved us from lead poisoning), and the figures were cast from molten lead poured into carbon black coated molds. With a little practice, we turned them out by the hundreds and mounted great cowboy and Indian cavalry skirmishes. The tiny bit of lead supplied in the kit didn't last long and we raided our father's supply of house flashing. When this was exhausted, we stripped lead flashing already installed in the house. Another, "Thrashing of your life," trip to the barn became necessary when unexpected house leaks appeared.

Recently, I told one of my teenage grandsons these stories about our spare time activities, when we were his age. He said, "Wow, how did you find the time to do all those things? Of course, you were lucky; you didn't have television, video games and the Internet to take up your time." I thought about this reaction a bit and then decided, "Yes, we were pretty darn lucky."

CHAPTER 20

THE CLUBHOUSE SET

 group of neighborhood boys form the Windmill
Literary Society, Eastham Haymow Stamp
Club and other exclusive Cape Cod clubs.

There was hardly a time when the neighborhood gang
wasn't busy establishing or disbanding a club. We had a
variety of motivating forces—a suitable clubhouse and an
insatiable appetite for chocolate bars in one, admiration of the
comic book hero Doc Savage in another and in a third, stamp
collecting.

The first of these clubs was founded when several of
us—my brother Fenton, cousin Ken Mayo and next door
neighbors, Bill and Bob Watson and Monk Wilson—were
exploring the millstone and auxiliary equipment beneath the
boarded up windmill located on what is now Eastham's
Windmill Green. Fenton hit his head on the flooring above
and noticed a trap door. He climbed through the opening and
the rest of us swarmed after him.

The mill had been built 300 years ago to grind wheat and
corn in the days when Eastham was called the "Breadbasket
of Massachusetts." It had a rich, musty, grainy aroma mixed

Town Hall and Old Mill, Eastham, Mass.

Eastham's wind powered gristmill in the 1920's.

with the scent of oak timbers. We explored the first floor grinding equipment and the second floor with its giant wooden gears, which transferred the wind's energy from the sails to the millstone. We especially liked the warm, dry room at

the third level, under the conical roof adjacent to the main shaft connected to the windmill's arms. A small window provided light and we could also observe the outside world from our 30-foot aerie without danger of detection. It made an ideal secret meeting place, the perfect clubhouse.

Next we had to find a rationale for a club. We spent a lot of time collecting "tonic," (New England-ese for soda), bottles by the roadside, and exchanging them for candy bars at Barton's store. Clark's Bolster Bars were popular, but the favorite was Mr. Goodbar, a Depression-era chocolate bar which offered twice as much candy for the money. On a good Saturday, we accumulated more Mr. Goodbars than we could comfortably digest, and our newly found clubhouse was a good place to store the surplus. In addition, the Eastham Public Library was only a few hundred feet down the road. On our free Saturdays, we took the allowed three books from the Library as soon as it opened, read them in our little room under the windmill's roof while maintaining our energy with a few candy bars, and then exchanged the books for another three at closing time.

Eastham Public Library probably soon after its construction in 1903(?)

After several months of reading our way through the Hardy Boys, Rover Boys and Tom Swift while gorging on chocolate, we lost our meeting place. The town fathers decided to refurbish the mill and open it to the public as a tourist attraction. Close to 70 years later, the mill is still open and on a recent visit, I was disappointed to discover that the ladder up to our alcove was gone. I had hoped to find a few leftover Mr. Goodbar wrappers there, souvenirs of the Windmill Literary and Chocolate Gourmand Society.

A year later, we formed another toney literary club. Tom Swift and his ilk were passé: now we were addicted to the pulps, those low cost monthly magazines with titles such as *Argosy, Astounding Science Fiction, Wild West Adventure, The Shadow* and *Doc Savage.* Doc was our favorite, a combination of Lamont Cranston, (aka The Shadow), Superman, and Spiderman, a debonair socialite who devoted his life to correcting injustices. Two pals assisted him: Ham, an incredibly clever lawyer who sported a cape and a sword cane, and Monk, (no connection with our Monk), a huge athletic and powerful man with an encyclopedic knowledge of all the physical sciences. There might have been a girlfriend, but the author knew his pre-teenage audience and kept her role to a minimum. Doc was the leader and as knowledgeable and muscular as his cohorts.

In their performance of daring, technical and nearly impossibly outrageous feats, the trio were precursors to James Bond. Trapped in a hopeless situation, one might pull at a loose thread on his coat and, behold, a spider web—thin, unbreakable strand on which they could climb to safety. Another would dislodge a false tooth filled with a corrosive, lock-destroying acid; or pivot a hinged shoe heel to disclose a coiled, carbide-coated wire, which would saw through hardened steel as though it were salami. After a few months, our parents declared Doc off limits because he was interfering with our studies.

The longest-lasting club, and one of the few non-secret societies, was devoted to stamp collecting. Our first meeting place, the Mayo family haymow, gave us a name—the Eastham Haymow Stamp Club. In a few weeks we moved to an unused chicken coop behind the Sparrow garage. We narrowly escaped being the Eastham Chicken Coop Stamp Club.

Some of the Eastham Haymow Stamp Club members. George Rongner and Donald Sparrow standing, Bob Watson, Bill Watson and Ken Mayo kneeling.

This highly structured club lasted two years. We collected dues, held regular meetings complete with minutes of the previous one, and staged a fundraising variety show featuring a cornet duet by brothers Robert and Fenton: "In a Little Gypsy Tea Room," every other note off-key, Fenton now recalls. A magic act by Bob Watson and a snappy Joe Miller blackface comedy routine filled out the bill. Our one performance in the chicken coop was well attended, but there was no popular outcry for a repeat. At five cents a head, our fundraiser was a bust anyway.

Seeking wider recognition for the active club, our president, George Rongner, wrote to President Roosevelt, inviting him to be an honorary member. Missy LeHand, FDR's secretary, sent a gracious response, telling us that the President was pleased with the honor and deeply appreciated our thinking of

THE WHITE HOUSE
WASHINGTON

October 11, 1933.

My dear Master George:

The President was delighted to receive the very nice letter which you and the members of your club sent to him and has asked me to tell you how deeply he appreciates your thought of him.

Very sincerely yours,

M. A. LeHand

M. A. LeHAND
Private Secretary

Master George Rongner,
Eastham Haymow Stamp Club,
Eastham,
Massachusetts.

Letter acknowledging President Roosevelt's acceptance of honorary membership in the E.H.S.C.

him. I hope that she did tell him about the invitation and that he really was delighted with his appointment as honorary member of the Eastham Haymow Stamp Club, at a time, in the depths of the Depression, when he needed a chuckle.

CHAPTER 21

THE GREAT ACORN WARS

 reat oaks from little acorns really doth grow.

Whatever the status and membership of our clubs when October came, all allegiances were forgotten as the great acorn wars raged. The origin of the wars, like that of most wars, is lost in the mists of time. However, when the acorns began to collect under the white oaks in our Nauset neighborhood, we felt an irresistible urge to do battle, using acorns and slingshots as the tools of war. Most of the Nauset boys participated, the four in my family, the two Watson boys, the younger Mayo boys, George Rongner, Monk Wilson, and an occasional ringer from the center of town.

We paid great attention to the construction of the slingshot. Green wood from an apple tree or arrowwood shrub growing on the bank of Uncle Dan's pond were preferred for the Y-shaped body. Such wood was strong and springy so one could impart a whip-like motion to the acorn. Rubber bands cut from an old inner tube and tied into grooves in the tops of the "Y" provided the propulsion power. Positioned in the

117

middle of the rubber bands was a square leather patch cut from the tongue of an old shoe. No two slingshots were alike; each boy had his own theory as to the best design and proudly defended the special configuration of his weapon—length of the handle, angle of the "Y," and diameter of the working fork, were some of the options.

Two schools of thought existed on the positioning of the oblong corn in the leather pocket, with its long axis vertical or, alternatively, horizontal, parallel to the ground. Some thought it possible to curve an acorn when launched in the horizontal position, while others held that a vertical acorn could be fired greater distances and more accurately. I tended to use one or the other, depending upon the circumstance, vertical when the enemy was hiding behind a tree, and horizontal when the target was far away.

The biggest acorns came from the oaks on the Warner property, a nearby summer home. Their huge English white oaks were said to have grown from acorns brought from South Africa. Ammunition was plentiful under the horizontal branches reaching as much as 40 feet from a two-foot-diameter trunk. One tree in particular produced enormous acorns, some over two inches long and one inch thick, the biggest of any found here and we saved these for the heavy artillery.

The first suitable autumn Saturday, we chose up sides, a lengthy and sometimes acrimonious process. Wilbur and Robert, the oldest and strongest, were usually the captains. Everyone wanted Whit Howes, (a ringer from the center of town), or Carleton Mayo, who were the best athletes. Neither captain was anxious to get the smaller boys, especially Bob Watson who had a bad habit of losing his temper in the heat of battle. The teams next collected several buckets of acorns and selected a main fortress, an abandoned farm outbuilding or a dense group of trees.

The objective of the battle was the same as in a snowball fight: dislodge the enemy from his fixed position. Capture of a strong point didn't end the war; we held secondary positions in reserve. However, we were careful to protect the buckets of acorns because loss of the ammunition was a fatal blow. With pockets stuffed with acorns and opportunities to restock frequently, the action could last for two or three hours. Almost always, the end of formal hostilities was triggered by someone, usually Bob, losing his temper and attacking with fists, rather than acorns. At other times, the accusation that a stone had been substituted for an acorn led to the fights, occasionally with some justification. An acorn hit on clothing stung, while contact with bare flesh raised a lump and left a bruise. A stone would beak the skin, and so a show of blood was considered strong evidence that illegal stones had been put into play.

The acorn wars raged over a considerable part of the real estate around our farm, the adjacent fields and Cedar Bank Links. Mostly open fields at the time, the area is now heavily wooded with cedars, pines and oaks, some of them white oaks. I like to think that the largest ones grew from flying acorns, planted with a slingshot 60 years ago.

CHAPTER 22

CAPE COD RUMRUNNERS

*H*igh speed boats manned by neighbors of the Sparrow family bring in the good stuff from Rum Row.

We weren't the only ones to put Eastham's shoreline to good use. During Prohibition, rumrunners landed thousands of cases of contraband liquor along the coast of Cape Cod. The Eighteenth Amendment to the Constitution, ratified in 1920, made it illegal to manufacture, sell, transport, export or import alcoholic beverages—defined as any liquid containing more than one-half of one percent alcohol. This "Noble Experiment" required all Americans, among the highest per capita consumers of liquor in the world, to become teetotalers with the stroke of a pen.

A large portion of the population spent much time and energy over the next 13 years trying to circumvent this idealistic law. Cape Codders were no exception. Production of homemade wine and beer was commonplace. As in many homes, a five-gallon crock behind the stove, emitting a yeasty/musty aroma, was standard equipment in our kitchen. Father had access to three 50-gallon barrels of wine, laid down for Mr. Shaw, that sat behind locked doors in golf course buildings. Stores carried yeast preparations with labels spelling out in some detail the consequences, "If yeast were to fall into a vat of grape juice and allowed to remain for several days in the absence of air users should be aware that the resulting beverage would be strictly illegal."

An army of professionals rose to supplement the trickle of alcohol produced by these enthusiastic amateurs. Rumrunners who brought top quality liquors of all types from offshore sources were regarded as the elite of the professionals. Bootleggers were at the lower end of the social spectrum. Their product, "bathtub" gin, was made from alcohol of questionable parentage and the quality ranged from adequate to awful, and occasionally lethal.

Bud Cummings in 1985. In his youth, one of Eastham's rumrunners.

We believed that our next door neighbor, Bud Cummings, was a rumrunner, because sometimes late at night, we observed his front window shade go up and down three times after which a heavily loaded truck lumbered down his long driveway and unloaded a lot of large bundles. Just before Bud died in 1993, I conducted an oral history interview with him and he freely and happily discussed his rumrunning days.

A typical rumrunning boat.

The U.S. Paulding is a "four piper" destroyer.

He worked for a Boston businessman who operated a 50-foot speed boat out of Scituate Harbor—a light, open, wooden structure, powered by three, 650-horsepower Garwood engines. At full throttle speed of 55 knots, it was capable of outrunning any Navy or Coast Guard vessel.

Bud reported for work every day, just as for a conventional, four to midnight job, and played cards to while away the time until the call came to pick up a load of cases. The four or five man crew would be given half of a U.S. greenback to be matched with the other half held by the delivering agency. A five dollar half might be good for 500 cases. They motored beyond the 12 mile limit to an area known as Rum Row, 20 to 30 miles northeast of Provincetown. Coastal vessels, usually French of St. Pierre and Miquelin origin and loaded with contraband spirits, waited there for the high-speed boats.

The liquor was generally delivered in packs of 12 one-quart bottles, wrapped in straw and sewed into a burlap bag with protruding ears. With the scene illuminated by the searchlights of federal ships that could observe but not interfere, the crew quickly transferred their cases to the 50-foot boat. Machine gun-armed French sailors hung from the rigging of the larger ship to guard against hijackers, not the U.S. vessels. When fully loaded, the rumrunner's boat took off at top speed and quickly outdistanced any pursuers.

Now their concern was landing the cargo at a safe place. The outer Cape had a number of attractive sites—Boat Meadow, First Encounter Beach, Pamet River, Indian Neck and Rock Harbor, to name a few—which were suitable for landing a load of cases. Boats were met by an unloading crew and the cases transferred to the "drop," an unused barn or summer cottage. Bud's crew liked the West Dennis breakwater area because it was isolated and the local officials were not too demanding. He reported that the offloading crew sometimes included a few State Troopers and the drop was owned by a local town official.

Not all the rumrunning operations went as smoothly as this. A boat might get hung up on the flats and need to jettison a number of cases, or might be intercepted close to shore by a Coast Guard vessel and be forced to throw over the entire cargo. Many boat owners learned to tie the cases together in a line and kick the lead case overboard when the Coast Guard got too close. The last case was attached to a buoy and the rumrunner could return at his convenience and retrieve his whiskey. Sometimes, a cake of salt was used to sink the buoy. After a couple of days in the water, the salt would have dissolved enough to allow the buoy to pop to the surface, well after the Coast Guard boat had left the scene.

Word of cases being jettisoned onto the flats spread quickly, and residents armed with rakes lost no time in making their way to the area. One of Eastham's senior citizens, Art Nickerson, reports that once when coming home from school, he was greeted by his mother with, "Don't stop, get down to South Sunken Meadow, there's a load of booze ashore." He reports that he financed his Washington trip and bought his first car with the proceeds of that afternoon.

Anyone recovering bottles or cases didn't have to search for a buyer. In Art Nickerson's words, "You didn't waste time sitting around the table wondering how to get rid of it. A knock on the door, (sometimes you didn't know whether to open it or not), and there would be a customer." A bottle of champagne was a particularly happy discovery. Money from the sale of one quart would pay for a tank of gas for his jalopy and two tickets to a high school dance.

Prohibition gave the shaky Cape economy a real boost. Bud Cummings and his boat crew shared five dollars for every case brought ashore and he guessed that they landed about 40,000 cases over a three year period. It's impossible to determine the total amount of liquor landed on Cape shores during Prohibition. One source estimates two million cases or ten million dollars for bringing it in from Rum Row. This at a time when the typical laborer earned 25 cents an hour.

A bottle of Prohibition days Log Cabin Bourbon dredged from Cape Cod Bay in the 1990's.

Draggers today occasionally find a bottle of the good stuff in their nets. A young Eastham quahogger, Dana Richardson, showed me a brown pint bottle he had recovered from the Bay a few years ago. It is filled with liquid, the closure and cork still intact and the words Old Log Cabin Bourbon molded into the glass. According to Bud Cummings, Old Log Cabin was a high quality, popular Prohibition whiskey.

Dana's father, a Prohibition days quahogger who dabbled in rumrunning, told me that after 20 years or so, the sea water starts to penetrate the cork and the whiskey is "off." I like to believe that the cork on this particular bottle is still sound and when Dana opens it I want to be there to sip a 65-year old bourbon, a souvenir of Cape Cod's rumrunning past.

CHAPTER 23

EASTHAM YELLOWBELLIES

astham's students from "across the tracks" attend Orleans High, take dancing lessons for the Senior Prom and embark on the highly anticipated senior class trip to Washington.

One of the crosses borne by Eastham students attending the old Orleans High School was frequent exposure to a rather rude couplet:

Eastham yellowbelly go for a swim?
Yes by God, when the tide comes in!

I grew up thinking that the rhyme referred to the color of our yellow schoolhouse. Recently, an Orleans classmate told me that "yellowbelly" came from the color of the belly of a freshly opened quahog, and the ditty implied that a steady diet of the shellfish had led Eastham residents to adopt some elements of its life style. The rhyme was unfair—my brothers and I were no strangers to quahogs but the mollusk was far from our sole source of nourishment.

In any case, we had more than enough problems already. The six of us who graduated in 1933 from that little yellow schoolhouse (I in my cut-down blue serge suit) felt lost in this large school with over 100 students. In addition, Eastham was "across the tracks" in the eyes of Orleans people. The sense of confusion and concern for the unknown that Monk and I felt was compounded by our tender ages and lack of social as well as physical maturity. However, we gained a measure of confidence in ourselves, and respect from the Orleans students, when we both scored one hundred percent on our first math test. The teacher suspected collusion, but when we were able to prove we had not cheated, we became 24-hour sensations as the "brains from Eastham."

The principal, like his Eastham grade school counterpart, had a reputation as a strict disciplinarian. Mr. Herbert (Pop) Stewart had been recruited 20 years before, when the rugged farmer and fishermen students had given the previous principal a rough time. We all knew the story of his first day on the Orleans job. Put to the test with a shower of spitballs, he ordered the biggest of the boys to come to the front of the room. The six-footer refused and so Pop Stewart marched down, picked him up, screwed-to-the-floor desk, chair and all, and carried him forward. No more spit balls or serious discipline problems.

When I got to high school, Pop Stewart was still heavily muscled and powerful, a tall portly man in his late 50's. Even 20 years later, he sometimes lost control of his explosive temper and grabbed a male troublemaker and pushed him about. Once he threw Wilbur down a flight of stairs. Most of the time though, he was gentle and courteous and he always looked a bit sheepish after an outburst. He was also a good administrator, a fine teacher and a learned gentleman. He tried to persuade me to continue Latin and study Greek in college; in his mind, a knowledge of these languages was essential to a properly rounded education.

Orleans High School in 1920's.

The high school building was an ungainly, two-story structure with yellow asphalt shingles, rusty red trim and black iron fire escapes. As in Eastham, the boys and girls used separate entrances. Separation of the sexes extended even to the homerooms and we didn't get a chance to sit next to a girl except in the smaller classrooms. The lot across the street served as a baseball diamond and the basketball team played on a court over the town movie theater, which was housed in a 50-year-old wooden building.

School discipline problems were minor in comparison with the horror stories of today. Alcohol and drugs were unheard of on school grounds, and the rule against smoking was generally obeyed. Most students had a lively interest in, and curiosity about, the opposite sex, but separation of boys and girls made exploration of the subject difficult, (although not impossible), during school hours.

Such awful transgressions as whispering in class, rough-housing, inattention or impudence were met with the threat of being kept after school or, rarely, suspension. To be kept after school was a particularly ominous threat to the Eastham pupils because we missed the bus and had to walk, or hitch-hike, five miles to get home. Wilbur was hitchhiking home after being disciplined for fighting, when a junior high school teacher stopped and offered him a ride, but first she asked why he was walking. On being told the reason she said, "Well, I guess you had better keep on walking."

The important social events of the last two years at high school were the Junior Hop and Senior Prom, and social pressures made it impossible to avoid them. A number of the Eastham contingent didn't know how to dance and as the Senior Prom approached, we asked a local housewife, Mrs. Harriet Crosby, to teach us the basic steps. She agreed, but may have regretted her decision, as she struggled with the collection of awkward, tone-deaf novices. We practiced to the beat of only one tune, "I'm Going to Sit Right Down and Write Myself a Letter," perhaps because she didn't want to subject us to unnecessary surprises by changing the tempo.

Close to 60 years later, hearing the sound of the first few bars of this song instantly transports me back to the Crosby living room, moving woodenly with Mrs. C. in my timid embrace and counting, "One, two, three, four; one, two —" She was too good a teacher; I can manage a presentable fox trot, but to this day I can't waltz, the count isn't complete without the four.

Mrs. Crosby didn't make me into a Fred Astaire, but I felt sufficiently confident to at least ask a girl to my Senior Prom. I didn't exactly have an exclusive date for the dance. Monk, who had just turned 16, had a Model T Ford and his driving license. The two of us had been socializing with a Chatham girl, Toni Rollins, and we both escorted her to the Prom. Her mother must have encouraged, or insisted on, this dual escort system, because neither of us ever got a chance to be alone with her.

Cape Cod high school dances in the 1930's were as predictable as the sunrise. Ribbons and streamers in the class colors decorated the hall, dozens of multi-colored balloons hung in nets from the ceiling and colored lights were positioned around the periphery of the hall. Orchestras played only fox trots or waltzes. At 11 o'clock the members of the class and their dates, followed by the other couples, paraded the length of the floor in the Grand March, to the strains of "Pomp and Circumstance."

At one a.m. the overhead lights dimmed, (and at midnight on Saturdays; there was no dancing on the Sabbath), the orchestra swung into "I'll See You In My Dreams" featuring a syrupy, throbbing, tenor sax, and the balloons were released to float down among the slowly rotating lights onto the couples below.

Our date that night was stunning, in a full-length, plum-colored, velvet dress, exuding the aroma of Tweed perfume. Monk and I managed to survive the evening thanks to the mostly medium-slow fox trots and some sympathetic guidance from Toni. All three of us were nervous. I couldn't put two meaningful words together, and she relied much too heavily on the conversational impact of "definitely." She still gets top marks for putting up with our awkward foxtrot.

The single most important pre-graduation event of our high school careen came the spring of our senior year, the Washington trip. This was the only time that most Cape Codders ever left New England and the first time that many had ridden on a train, stayed in a hotel or been away from home without parental supervision. Our class was chaperoned by Pop Stewart and the biology teacher, Miss Doris Trowt. He had accompanied every class for the last 20 years, and loved the duty. The famous temper remained in Orleans, and he managed to miss or overlook all but the most flagrant misbehavior. Also, he was much too busy to pay a lot of attention to his charges. An attractive, middle-aged lady joined our group in New York, and Mr. Stewart, a bachelor, spent most of the time remaining escorting her about.

We traveled by bus to Boston and then boarded the overnight, Eastern Steamship Line's ship to New York City. A *New Bedford Standard Times* newspaper account describes the departure, " —a cavalcade of automobiles carrying parents, relatives and friends, who were on hand to bid the group bon voyage, left for the Cape Cod Canal and lined the shores waving goodbye to the ship as it steamed through the Canal three hours later." The trip through the canal and the final exchange of goodbyes seemed to signal a release of parental control, a rite of passage to adulthood. Not that we indulged in wild debauchery. For me, exploring this new freedom took the form of smoking a mentholated cigarette and betting on miniature horses as they were moved along the deck according to the roll of dice.

After dinner in New York's Taft Hotel the following evening, most of the boys headed for Minsky's Burlesque Theater, (not yet closed down by Mayor LaGuardia). We took pains to leave the hotel separately, under a variety of excuses, and then rendezvous at the theater so as to escape observation by Mr. Stewart. These moves were really unnecessary; a subsequent class reported seeing him in the theater, enjoying the show immensely. As we presented our tickets, the doorman looked at me suspiciously and asked, "How old are you?" I was only 15 and had shaved for the first time when preparing for the trip. Standing as tall as I could I said in what was intended to be a bass voice, "Twenty-one." To my embarrassment, it came out in a high-pitched falsetto. He laughed and

Orleans High School class of 1937 in Washington. Donald Sparrow, second from right, "Monk" Wilson, seventh from right, Pop Stewart, second from left.

waved us all in to the theater. My memory is that Gypsy Rose Lee was the featured performer. At the time, we felt sinful, but in truth, the jokes and the dancing were less risqué than most television shows today.

Boys and girls were quartered on separate floors in both the New York and Washington hotels. Knowing this in advance, Monk Wilson and I had spent hours developing a strategic plan to get to the girls' floor, (or to get the girls to our floor), and avoid the chaperone protecting his or her charges. One element of our plan, a product of Monk's fertile imagination, involved courting the good will of the elevator operators by tipping them liberally so that when we lured a girl into his cage, they would wink as we exited at the girls' floor. They must have thought us loony. I told Otto Nickerson about one scheme when we chatted. He asked if it had worked. It didn't and we probably wouldn't have known what to do if it had worked.

After the Washington trip there was little to do except wait for graduation and look for a job. College Boards were not offered to us, and none of us realized their importance if we were thinking of college. It was not the best time to go forth into the world. The country was still in a deep Depression and Hitler was rampaging about Europe, setting the stage for another world war. None of this concerned us, with the naïvety and optimism of youth; we believed that in completing high school, we had survived the worst that life could throw at us. Would that this optimism could have been justified.

CHAPTER 24

THE MODEL T AND OTHER JALOPIES

*T*he author discovers the joys of a rumble seat and the drawbacks of a 1932 Essex.

Much of our teenage spare time was spent working on an old wreck of a car: Model T or Model A Ford, 1932 Essex, to name a few, trying to restore it to running condition or struggling to merely keep it going. My familiarity with the former came from our mechanically gifted next-door neighbor and cousin, Carleton Mayo. Just being around him I absorbed a sizeable body of knowledge on the art of caring for and handling a Model T. Even the smallest kids knew, for example, that the motor frequently back-fired when starting and so you should crank with your thumb tucked into your palm and follow through when finishing the stroke, so as to get your hand and arm out of the way. A backfire caused the crank to kick back violently and break a carelessly placed thumb or wrist.

Carleton frequently asked bystanders to operate the spark and gas levers (located on the steering column) while he cranked. The motor usually caught with a few scattered explosions, increasing in frequency until it smoothed out to a full-throated roar. The trick in operating the levers was to resist the temptation to cut back after the first few explosions, but rather to wait until the motor was turning over at a satisfactory rate before retarding the throttle. If we did our job well, we were rewarded with a ride, usually through the open fields, since Carleton owned his Model T for two or three years before getting his driver's license. The car had large wheels and plenty of road clearance so we took off across the open fields as though we were on a horse, but at a considerably faster clip.

Gas was always in short supply, and so ways of extending our meager supply was a continuing subject for discussion. Some believed that the addition of mothballs to the tank would increase both the gas mileage and the engine's horsepower. The only time I saw this tried, dense clouds of black smoke poured from the exhaust. Maybe we had the wrong kind of mothballs. Sometimes, we substituted household kerosene for gasoline, but had to start the motor on the standard fuel and then shift over to kerosene. It worked fine, except for two problems—the exhaust fumes would create an EPA red alert in today's world, and after running for a while on the new fuel, the motor became so hot it continued to run even with the ignition off. The only way to stop the motor was to cut off the supply of fuel. I was once with a Boston-based friend of the family who became stuck in a Sumner Tunnel traffic jam with no way to interrupt the flow of kerosene. He was the most unpopular man in Boston as the unstoppable motor filled the Tunnel with its hideous fumes.

The connection between the motor and wheels was a somewhat mysterious mechanism based entirely on friction, called a planetary system. This, as well as the braking system, involved the use of "bands" that broke when subjected to unusual stresses. Carleton's practice when the brake band failed, (as it did frequently), was to throw the car into reverse to stop it. Sometimes the reverse band let go too and this left him, literally, freewheeling with no means of slowing down or stopping except for a sharp rise in the road or a field.

Our older brother Robert was the first in our family to get his own car, a bottle green Model A Ford convertible roadster with a rumble seat. The last cars with rumble seats were made in the 30's and now even the term has just about disappeared from the vocabulary of anyone under the age of 50. I learned this sad fact during a coffee-break conversation with a young secretary in our office years ago when I boasted that as a youngster I had been the rumble seat rassling champion of outer Cape Cod. She destroyed me with, "What's a rumble seat?"

For the benefit of the unfortunate young, a rumble seat was fitted into the back of a roadster and became invisible when the lid was closed. Opened, it turned into a cozy recess with seats just barely wide enough to accommodate two people. The rider's upper torso was completely exposed to the car's slipstream—a miniature tornado when going at a good clip. In winter, especially with rain or snow, it was a cruel and unforgiving place. However, in warm weather with clear skies and a full moon, it was delightful, a great encouragement to young romance. George Bernard Shaw's characterization of marriage as offering the maximum of temptation with the maximum of opportunity comes to mind.

My own first car was not a Ford, but a prestigious, 1932 Essex. Fenton and I bought it in 1938 for $25. A four-door sedan with rich, plush seats, polished hardwood inside trim and a dent- and rust-free exterior, it seemed a terrific buy. It was beautiful but unfortunately, the $25 price tag gave a clue as to its mechanical condition. Problems appeared quickly.

Our 1932 Essex, purchase price in 1938, $25.

The driver's door had a defective latch and we learned to hold onto it when making a right turn. The horn had died, and a bugle became a permanent fixture on the dashboard. Fenton played the trumpet and so took care of the warning system, giving a good blast on the bugle even while maneuvering at high speed.

The motor proved to be close to junk. It literally burned as much oil as gas, and so we were forced to carry gallon jugs of crankcase oil in the trunk. Top speed of 45 miles per hour was achieved only downhill, and with a good tail wind. The motor didn't like to start and we had to remove two of the four spark plugs and pour gasoline into the cylinders to get it to turn over.

This jalopy finally met its end one evening when Fenton discovered that the gas tank was leaking large amounts of gas. No gas stations were open and he decided that the best bet was to drive at top speed so as to cover the five miles to home as quickly as possible. As he clunked along at 45 miles per hour, he heard a loud bang and the heap came to a shuddering halt. The drive shaft had become detached and, as it fell to the ground, wiped out a number of essential operating elements of the car. He and his friends pushed it to its final resting place, the fields behind our barn.

Recently, I found its rusted remains where it had been deposited 60 years ago. In a nostalgic mood, I salvaged some of the hardwood windshield trim intending to sand it and install it over our fireplace mantel. This idea led to some spirited discussion in our household.

"It will be a wonderful conversation piece."

"Yes, that's what we are afraid of."

As soon as I find the answer to that one, I will reopen the campaign to display the relic of my first love, the 1932 Essex.

CHAPTER 25

THE SMELL OF MONEY

kunks are caught and processed by the "King of the Skunkers"

Honeysuckle and rambling roses in June, salt breezes off the ocean, scrub pines in hot sunlight, freshly-cut cedar trees. These are a few of the fragrances which take me back to Cape Cod in the 1930's. But the most effective reminder is the pungent aroma of a skunk under attack. Unpleasant to many, to me and my friends it was a welcome odor, the smell of money. Selling skunk hides helped to keep many of us solvent during the fall and winter months.

We trapped the skunks or simply collected them as they foraged at night. The most successful and persistent of our youthful skunkers was our next-door neighbor, Charlie Escobar, who preferred to track them down on foot. In his teens, he gathered as many as 150 pelts a year in this fashion.

Ideal skunking conditions called for a full moon with no wind to blow away the scent. A good skunking dog was essential, one good at spotting skunks and smart enough to stay clear and avoid getting sprayed, or "scented," as Charlie delicately put it. His Prince, a mutt with strong fox terrier ancestry, was expert at locating skunks and equally adept at keeping a safe distance. Other essentials for his type of night skunking were a flashlight, a burlap bag, a change of clothes and an assistant, usually one of my older brothers.

Skunks discourage their foes by squirting a fine stream of liquid from sacs located under the tail. When spotted by Prince, who stood a discreet ten to twelve feet away, the skunk kept its eyes fixed on the dog, tail arched, ready to turn and squirt. The skunk can squirt only when its paws are planted firmly on something solid like the ground. Once the skunk was preoccupied by the dog, one of the team, generally my brother, held a flashlight on the animal while the fearless skunker ran behind and quickly picked it up by the tail in one rapid, continuous, motion. If this operation was not performed expertly, the lifter became thoroughly "scented." Once safely off the ground, the skunk was popped into the burlap bag while the crew stood up wind.

Charlie Escobar in 1980, in his youth the King of the Skunkers.

Charlie was absolutely fearless when moving in for a live capture, or for the kill. As a result, an unmistakable aroma clung to him during the entire skunking season. In his late teens he took to smoking vicious, black, curly Italian Piroques (stogies), which altered the character of the aroma, but not necessarily for the better. We speculated that Charlie might have inspired Al Capp's comic strip character, "Inside man at the skunk works."

Being sprayed had its advantages. Our grammar school principal couldn't tolerate the aroma and would ask the scented ones to go home until the smell became less offensive. If emanations from his clothing failed to free him from the humdrum school routine, Charlie found that a shoe placed next to the coal-fired, pot-bellied stove guaranteed prompt dismissal.

The legal skunking season lasted from October to April, the period when the furs were in prime condition with thick hair firmly attached to the hides. But Charlie extended the season a bit by capturing skunks before cold weather set in and keeping them alive until the season opened. He stock-piled them in cages under his barn, as many as 25 to 30 skunks, living happily on table scraps.

After the skunks had been dispatched, with a swift blow from a baseball bat, the real work began. The skins had to be peeled, intact, from the carcass, salted and stretched, inside out, over a boat-shaped form whittled from a shingle. The economic realities of our skunking endeavors didn't allow the luxury of the commercial wire forms, sold by Sears Roebuck.

Charlie saved the fat from the carcass and tried it out to recover the grease. He reported that fried bits of the meat tasted very much like chicken, no skunky flavor at all. Cape Codders thought that the grease had great medicinal value, used externally or internally. The best thing for a chest cold was a thick layer of skunk grease overlaid with a flannel cloth, to keep it nice and warm. Some mothers made a mixture called "lemon oil," (grease diluted with lemon extract), and used it as cough medicine. One patient observed, "She called it lemon oil, but we smelled pretty strong for a while."

Boston furriers or itinerant brokers bought our dried pelts. Predominantly black furs, "quarter stripers," commanded top price, $2.50 for a large one. Furs with more white brought a lower price and "full stripers" were worth as little as 25 cents. We regarded the brokers as overly sharp busi-nessmen with numerous reasons for downgrading what we regarded as top-notch pelt. Our visions of affluence dimmed as the broker reeled off his price-reducing ploys—our quarter striper was really a half striper, the hides had not been stretched, dried or stored properly, the skunk had been consumptive and so the hair was scanty, the skunk had been the loser in a bad fight, and so on.

The demand for skunk fur coats disappeared after World War II. In any case, teenagers could make money in other, and easier, ways in the post-war economy, but none of them nearly as exciting, or aromatic, as skunking.

CHAPTER 26

THE STAND

*T*he author works hard and lives the good life at the first franchised Howard Johnson stand.

To anyone who lived or summered on the outer Cape in the 1930's and 40's, "The Stand" means only one thing—the Howard Johnson's restaurant at the intersection of Routes 6 and 28 in Orleans, the first franchised Ho Jo stand in the country. Howard Johnson owned and operated a number of restaurants in the Boston area in the early 1930's, but this was the first, franchised Howard Johnson's stand. In the mid-1930's he made an agreement with his longtime friend and Quincy neighbor, Reggie Sprague, to use the Howard Johnson name and products in an owner-operated restaurant. According to his daughters, Jean and Barna, there was no written agreement. A handshake closed the deal that became the model for thousands of franchised Howard Johnson restaurants around the world.

The unique characteristics which set the Howard Johnson stands apart from other roadside restaurants were already in place: orange roof, Simple Simon logo, 28 flavors of ice

The first francised Howard Johnson Stand, 1937.

cream, tender fried clams, lavish scoops of marvelously rich ice cream on a sugar cone or resting precariously on top of a soda glass and the ever-present, irresistible aroma of grilled frankfurters on a toasted bun. No wonder the Orleans stand was an immediate hit.

The Spragues worked together as a management team. He was an engaging, outgoing, rough and ready, story-telling World War I Navy veteran. A visored sailing hat was always perched on his head and everyone called him "Skipper." Purchasing, public relations and supervision of the kitchen and counter help were his duties. He projected a bull-of-the-woods image, but was really a soft touch, reluctant to fire anyone except under extreme provocation. He could pick up derogatory comments about himself, the job or the stand on an intercom between the kitchen and his upstairs office. When this happened, he returned the compliment, at length and in salty, enlisted sailors language. However, on a busy day with the help running around in a frenzy, he frequently came down with a fistful of dollar bills and handed them out to everyone in the kitchen. This, at a time when one dollar had the purchasing power of a present day 20 dollar bill.

After Labor Day, when the summer crowds had disappeared and business was slow, he often closed shop early and took the waitresses to the movies. He either fell asleep and snored loudly, or if it happened to be a sentimental Judy Garland movie, he sat with tears coursing down his cheeks.

We sometimes referred to Mrs. Sprague as Mother Sprague or Gladys, but it was always "Mrs." to her face. Her "bottomline" role counter-balanced the heart-of-gold Skipper. She supervised the waitresses and cashiers and kept a very careful eye on income and outgo.

The Stand was important to local youngsters because we found jobs there at a time when the U.S. unemployment rate for teens was over 25 percent. In addition, those lucky enough to be hired found that it was a fun place to work. The owners worked as hard as anyone, but they managed to create a relaxed and freewheeling environment. Most of the help were unmarried and there were lots of summer romances, many of which turned into marriages. Finally, with a little initiative, the help could eat even better than the customers.

In 1940, my first year, dishwashers and countermen were paid $14 a week, raised to $17 the next year, including meals. I started on the counter, but was quickly shifted to the kitchen. Any disappointment I felt at losing the "glamour" job disappeared when I learned that it was a lot more fun and we ate better in the kitchen, an important point because I needed enormous amounts of food to sustain the height and weight I put on during those summers. Our duties in the kitchen, other than washing dishes, pots and pans, included cleaning lobsters and chickens for salads, frying clams and peeling potatoes for French fries and mashed potatoes. Cooking and cleaning the lobster became my specialty. At first, I didn't dare eat any of the meat because my mother was allergic to lobster and I thought I would be ill. A little experimentation dispelled that concern and shortly it was one piece for Skipper and one for me, usually the most succulent, tender claw meat.

I spent a lot of time stroking the backs of the live lobsters, trying to get them to sit up on their tails. The lobsterman's wife, Mrs. Gertrude Hunt, who delivered them, told me about this trick and assured me that they would respond to the right touch. It never worked for me.

Our pay included nourishing meals, but soon I learned to augment the company food with more interesting fare. Tiring of lobster, I might admire the meat cutter's artistry and could count on him saying, "This tenderloin steak is too small to serve to the customers, why don't you have it for your lunch." He was also the custodian of the deep freeze where the five-gallon tins of ice cream were stored. A half-inch always protruded above the top of the new can, and he winked at our practice of slicing off the exposed ice cream with a hot knife and eating it on the spot. We might tease a friendly waitress to cut a piece of pie improperly so it couldn't be served or to make a mistake in a soda fountain order. Such errors were not discarded and the kitchen help fought for them.

Skipper had to be aware of our gourmandizing, but he objected only once. A six-foot, six-inch, teenage dishwasher who weighed about 140 pounds and had two hollow legs was found sitting on the cellar steps demolishing an entire boiled chicken. Skipper fired him on the spot and afterwards described him as "A skinny Charles Laughton doing Henry the Eighth."

Waitresses received the princely sum of $4.95 a week out of which they had to buy and maintain their own uniforms. The uniforms, calico or gingham dresses with a white starched apron tied in a big bow at the back, had to be fresh-ly laundered and the aprons starched and ironed at the start of every shift.

The kitchen help didn't really feel sorry for them. An attractive girl with a good figure could make as much as $60 a week in tips. The correlation between bust size and the magnitude of tips was a subject of considerable interest in the kitchen. One less-than-Reubenesque wait-ress bought and wore a set of spectacular falsies and claimed that her income doubled when she put them on. The

Dot Cummings, Reta's sister and a wait-ress at The Stand.

falsies had a rather obvious pair of nipples and attracted a great deal of attention from the kitchen crew. She tired of the comments after a week, removed the objects and, in full sight of everyone, cut off the nipples with a pair of kitchen shears. Several waitresses nearly fainted at the sight.

When a big spender came into the stand, the waitresses indulged in a certain amount of infighting. Clayton Mayo, a retired Singer Company executive who was known to leave a dollar tip after every meal, was one of the prized customers. Once when he came in, one waitress was heard to growl, "I would kill to get Clayton at my table."

Mother Sprague and Skipper had little trouble in staffing the stand. Jobs were scarce, so local youths and college students from all over the state fought for the opportunity. Nobody had to be bored. Beach parties, skinny-dipping in Crystal Lake and house parties were some of the after-hour activities. The traditional end to an evening was a ride to Hyannis for coffee at the Mayflower Café. Sometimes the next stop was the seven a.m. shift back at the stand. Provincetown was another favored late evening spot and on at least one occasion, Skipper had to post bail for some of his countermen when they became involved in a barroom brawl.

The off-Cape youngsters roomed in private homes or small rooming houses. One of the most popular for the boys was Ma Coffin's Elm Arch Lodge where they paid all of two dollars a week for rooms. Some of the free spirits drove Ma Coffin to distraction with their irresponsible behavior. On one occasion, Ben Mason and his friends tried to bring home a large potted palm they had liberated from a local bistro. Ma Coffin surveyed the giggling, stumbling gang from an upstairs window and mistaking the potted palm for a drunk, cried out, "You're not bringing him in here in that condition."

Non-paying guests were her particular bane. At any one time, she might have four or five freeloaders occupying rooms rented to one. Ben was a chronic offender, and she was after him constantly. One evening, having spent considerable time in the local bars, he decided he couldn't stand any more of her carping criticism and would have it out with her. He showered, combed his hair very carefully, put on a black bow tie and, naked as a jaybird, but with great dignity, walked downstairs and tried to explain his position to his landlady. She never raised the issue again and in fact, studiously avoided him as if he were dangerously mad.

Counterman was considered the glamour job. At that post, a young man got to meet and talk to the flocks of young female summer visitors. Also, at the start of the day, they looked sharp in their white shirts, black bow ties and waist length mess jackets. However, by the end of the shift, their uniforms resembled Jacob's coat, stained with blueberry pie,

The 1941 "Class Picture." The author, top row, far left, the Cummings sisters, Reta and Dot, third row, far left. Owners Gladys and Reggie Sprague, middle of second row. Jean Sprague, third row, second from right, Barna Sprague, first row, far right, Isabelle Richardson, second row, third from left, and Louise Fulcher, second row, third from right.

ketchup and many of the famous 28 flavors. The ice cream containers were kept directly behind the counter and during rush hour, with half a dozen countermen leaning over to scoop one of the 28, it was a sea of rumps. During the off-season, waitresses worked the counter. The coffee ice cream was stored in the hardest to reach container and one Lothario came in every evening to order a coffee cone and enjoy the leg show.

The cooks were mostly local people, permanent employees who provided a degree of stability and continuity to the kitchen staff. Isabelle Richardson, the pastry chef, was a quiet young woman with a delightfully dry sense of humor. Once, we were discussing one of the kitchen help whom she believed to be shy, but of questionable moral character. I observed that still waters run deep and she replied, "Yes, deep and dirty."

The head cook, Louise Fulcher, was an incurable matchmaker and responsible for many of the summer romances that blossomed into marriages. Louise, the Dolly Levi of the range, conspired to have her choice for me, an Orleans native, Reta Cummings, bring me a pan of hot milk and melted butter as I prepared mashed potatoes. The plan worked to perfection; Reta and I were married three years later.

We shared a sense of déjà vu when our younger son worked at the stand in the late 1960's, when the Spragues no longer owned it. We didn't recognize his description of the kitchen work, including all frozen, pre-packaged food, but one aspect of the job was consistent: he had two glorious summers surfing, sailing, beach-partying and romancing the waitresses.

CHAPTER 27

SUMMER COMPLAINTS

A native Cape Codder learns how to deal with summer visitors and even enjoy the company of some.

To native Cape Codders, the phrase "before the war" means only one thing, before World War II, before the year-round population exploded and before the Cape became a magnet for retirees. There were a lot fewer summer people then and they were different too—mostly well-to-do families living here while Papa commuted on weekends from Boston, or schoolteachers and college professors who found the Cape a pleasant and inexpensive place to enjoy the summer. They arrived en masse on the Fourth of July and departed just as suddenly on Labor Day. They appeared and disappeared at highly predictable times, and also seemed more worldly, better dressed, drove better cars and, we thought, tended to look down their noses at us.

We saw pretty much the same crowd every year, and so there were many opportunities for long-term relationships, but these rarely ripened to close, personal friendships. Attitudes on both sides, the natives and the "summer complaints" as we called them, ranged from cordial to cool tolerance.

When one of father's employers, and benefactors, summer resident Herbert Winslow died, the childless Mrs. Winslow took up residence in Boston's Ritz Carlton Hotel. We saw her once or twice a year when she rode into our driveway in the back seat of a chauffeured Pierce-Arrow automobile. Invariably, the chauffeur came into our house and asked our mother to come out to visit with Mrs. Winslow. The two chatted in the back seat for an hour or so, and then Mrs. Winslow was driven back to her Ritz Carleton suite. We didn't understand why Mrs. Winslow didn't come into our house. Mother was a good housekeeper and so she could not have had any concerns about cleanliness. Now I believe that the widow enjoyed mother's company but wanted the friendship to go just so far.

The long association between father and Mr. Shaw is another example of a warm native-city dweller relationship. Father worked for Mr. Shaw for over 20 years, and during that time, there were no strong disagreements or harsh words between the two men. Mr. Shaw gave father a completely free hand in managing the golf course workmen and the accounts, and the two conferred on technical details of running and improving the course.

Our family saw a lot of Mr. Shaw and his guests. His clubhouse had no telephone and so he and his guests used our phone for all their calls. They always treated us with great kindness when using our phone, or when my brothers and I took incoming messages up to the "big house." Between the adults, it was always Jennie or Dan and Mr. Shaw. They never socialized or discussed politics, sports, religion or engaged in relaxed small talk, yet this cordial but businesslike relationship survived much longer than many closer friendships or business associations could be expected to last.

Other employer relationships were less successful. Father did maintenance work for a vacation homeowner, Mr. Lowell we'll call him. Once I accompanied father on a call at Mr. Lowell's house to fix their gasoline-powered water pump motor. The master of the house hung at father's elbow, treating him to a rapid-fire stream of suggestions and questions. "Maybe it's out of gas, is the spark plug working, is that wire connected, is the magneto wet." Mrs. Lowell, seeing that father was about to blow his top, came to the rescue. About six inches taller than Mr. Lowell, she looked down at her husband and said sternly, "Charles, you go upstairs and don't come down until Dan has the pump running." As we left, the job completed, Mr. Lowell was leaning out the bedroom window waving and yelling, "Goodbye, Dan."

Younger Cape Codders also tended to deal at arms length with the summer visitors of the same age. Ed Brown of the Eastham Superette, a summer resident during the 1920's and 30's (now as much an Eastham native as anyone I know), explained to me that the natives always had to work and so organizing a ball game or swimming party was difficult. On occasions when the two groups got together for a baseball game, they didn't choose up sides, the city boys played the townies and both sides played to win.

When I was 14, a summer acquaintance of several years called to ask if I would camp out with him on Minister's Pond for a week. His attitude toward us natives had been somewhat patronizing—a real summer complaint—but I reluctantly agreed. We cleared the poison ivy from a spot on the shore (we didn't have a canoe and so couldn't use our peninsula camp), pitched pup tents, built a latrine, and were in business. Unfortunately, the rains started and continued unabated for four days. We ran out of food, the tents sprung hundreds of leaks, our bedrolls became sodden lumps, and we both grew very touchy. I don't recall the spark which touched off the skirmish, but it ended with each throwing the other's camping equipment into Minister's Pond, bedding and all. The next time we met, we were both married, and each of us attending graduate school. We managed a smile, but neither of us had any desire to reestablish the friendship.

Visitors assumed that Cape Codders were born with secretive, standoff-ish characteristics. When I was about ten, an off-Cape lady stopped me on what is now Route 6, to ask if a certain house in Eastham had been sold. She became angry when I replied that I, (honestly), really didn't know. She started in on me, "Oh come on, you Cape Codders are all the same, you know but you just won't talk to outsiders." She continued in this vein for at least five minutes before giving up and driving away. I was puzzled, but rather pleased, by the inference that I had been so astute in dealing with strangers.

Human nature and chemistry being what they are, summer romances between natives and city folk did occur. One of the most popular, if unlikely, meeting places, was the post office. By 7:30 in the evening, the parking lot of Abbie Nickerson's post office, (corner of Bridge and Samoset Roads), was crowded with teenager-loaded jalopies. Going for the evening mail was the 1930's equivalent of a non-alcoholic singles bar.

For at least two reasons, not many of the adolescent encounters developed into lasting relationships—the loved ones disappeared on Labor Day, and few of us natives had the time or money to drive off-Cape to press our case. Perhaps a more important inhibiting factor was the perceived economic and social gap. Cape Cod youths just weren't regarded as good catches by the summer visitor parents. While reminiscing with a number of my pre-War friends recently, none of us could think of a single, pre-War, summer romance that had led to marriage.

Despite the frustrations and frictions of dealing with the summer crowd, I looked forward to the annual July Fourth invasion. But the day after Labor Day, it was all over. The Cape returned to its quiet, slow pace and natives regained their privacy. For those of us who were teenagers, it was sometimes a bit lonely; we missed the companionship of the summer visitors, espe-  cially the opposite sex. One post-Labor Day Tuesday, I swam out to the raft anchored in Salt Pond. As happens so frequently early in September, the weather was perfect, a brilliant- ly clear, cloudless, blue sky, crisp, clean air and only a wisp of a breeze. I was alone on the raft surrounded by blue water, empty sky, blue-changing-to-green Nauset Bay and the silence broken only by an occasional car on the main road. Sadly, I thought, "Summer Complaints—you can't live with them and you can't live without them."

CHAPTER 28

ACROSS THE BRIDGE AND BACK

*T*he author leaves home for the first time to make his way in the world beyond Cape Cod.

When I graduated from high school, I was just barely 16. My parents thought I was too young to go to college. One of the Cedar Bank regulars and an Eastham summer resident, Mr. Matthew Luce, had been Registrar at Harvard, and was a good friend of the headmaster at Exeter Academy. He obtained a working scholarship for me at the prep school, and so off I went in the fall of 1937 to repeat my last year of high school. Exeter was light years away from Orleans High— academically, economically and socially. I was lost for the first three months and floundered for the next three, but managed by the end of the year to pass every course, except French. My grades were not college-worthy, and so Mr. Luce wangled another year of the working scholarship. This time, I passed with decent grades and did well enough on the college boards to qualify for a scholarship at Harvard.

The War had its impact on us even before Pearl Harbor. Wilbur, and then Robert, were drafted into the Army in 1941.

Wilbur

Robert

Fenton

Donald

The Sparrow brothers,
across the bridge in 1944.

Wilbur served in General George Patton's army as a staff sergeant, went through Europe, and when Germany surrendered, was sent to Okinawa to participate in the invasion of Japan. Fortunately, the war ended before that action was necessary. Robert was initially assigned to the Medical Corps, but transferred to the Air Corps after Pearl Harbor. He became a bomber pilot, flew 17 missions over Europe, and was lost when his plane, the Lambsy Divy, was hit by anti-aircraft fire and blew up over Hanover Germany in 1944.

Fenton had scholastic deferments until he enlisted in the Air Force in 1943, trained in fighter planes, and got his wings a year later. He spent the rest of the War in the States piloting fighter planes fitted with special protective armor, used as practice targets for machine gunners on bombers. They fired frangible bullets which, when on target, caused a light to flash in his cockpit, signaling a hit and the number of hits. Fenton called the planes, "flying pinball machines."

I too received scholastic deferments and after graduation from Harvard in 1943, had a variety of war related jobs: TNT production, chemist at Hooker Electro Chemical, and then assistant to Harvard Professor Robert B. Woodward on his total synthesis of Quinine project for Polaroid Corporation. I was deferred because all of these positions were considered vital to the war effort.

My years at Exeter and Harvard were both fortunate and unfortunate. I grew up a lot, but was absent when mother needed all the support she could get. All four sons were away from home and father's brain tumor had grown to the point where he was undergoing personality changes. He had continued to have excruciating headaches after Aunt Eva guessed his problem in 1928, but had managed to perform his job to Mr. Shaw's satisfaction. Now he started to have spells of uncontrolled anger and was not able to work at his previous level of competence. Meanwhile, his doctor was still treating him for a misdiagnosed sinus condition, instead of his far more serious and debilitating affliction.

His behavior finally became so bizarre that Mr. Shaw arranged for an examination at Mass General through a doctor who was one of the golf course regulars. The verdict: a well-advanced growth in the frontal lobe of his brain. After an eight-hour operation, the doctor told us that the benign tumor had invaded much of the frontal lobe. He had tried to remove only the multi-tentacled growth, but was forced to take some of the brain also.

A second operation, this time only five hours in length, was needed to complete the removal of the growth. My college roommate and I went up to dad's hospital room after the operation for a quick look-in, thinking he would be in no condition for visitors. We were amazed to find him trying to sit up in bed, his head swathed in a turban like bandage. He greeted us with, "Take this Goddamn thing off and get me a cigarette." We loosened the net designed to keep him from getting out of bed, while he lit up a cigarette and discussed events in a logical and rational fashion.

Despite these favorable signs, the operation left him with diminished capacity. He was able to drive a car, go for the mail, read the morning paper and discuss local happenings with the town's merchants, but he never worked again. He also acquired one unsettling habit. The doctors had removed a segment of his skull to gain access to the brain. They did not replace the quarter-moon shaped, three-by-five-inch, piece of bone after the operations, and so he had only a layer of skin protecting the diminished frontal area of his brain. He felt no pain when he massaged this deeply indented area of his head, as he did frequently, but strangers observing him sometimes remembered a pressing engagement.

Father lived another 12 years after the operation, perfectly happy in his somewhat childish state. But we remembered the vibrant, "hardest working man in town" before the operation and were saddened by thoughts of what might have been.

Before his operation, mother had to treat her husband very carefully, as she struggled with the terrible headaches, and it was not an easy time for her. When her four boys were in or beyond high school, she secured a part-time job as Eastham's first town accountant. She had always been good with numbers, easily solving the daily math puzzle in the *Boston Post*, (e.g., "If a train started from South Station at 40 miles per hour, etc.") Her stated purpose in working was to buy a good set of sterling flatware and to get father a pocket watch. These objectives were met over the next few years, but her real purpose may have been to enjoy her hobby and to give herself a break from her husband-sitting chore.

After father's operation, her life was different, but hardly better. Watching over his erratic behavior was a full-time job. Then came the War and Robert's death, when his plane was shot down over Germany. After father died of cancer in 1953, she was able to enjoy a few years of happiness with her son, Wilbur, living nearby. He had returned to Eastham after the War and worked in construction. Among the houses he built were two on Sparrow farmland, one for his family and another 100 yards down the road for his mother. He usually dropped in for a cup of coffee before work, and she greatly enjoyed his company. Sadly, she lost a second son when he died of a heart attack in 1963. She only lived another four years, believing that the hand Fate had dealt her was overly harsh.

Both Fenton and I worked in industry for 40 years and then retired to Orleans and Eastham, respectively. We had achieved our childhood ambition to escape from Cape Cod, but the three survivors of World War II couldn't stay away. We all learned that it's difficult to find any place across the bridge that's as pleasant as our side of the Cape Cod Canal.

SOURCES OF PHOTOS

All from the author's files with the exception of: